The Washington of the female propagandists

A balloon view from *Harper's Weekly*, July 27, 1861. The uncompleted Capitol dome seemed to the reformers symbolic of the unsatisfactory state of American democracy.

FEMALE PERSUASION

Six Strong-Minded Women

Margaret Farrand Thorp

ARCHON BOOKS
1971

Library of Congress Catalog Card Number: 74-150771
International Standard Book Number: 0-208-00999-X
The Shoe String Press, Inc., Hamden, Connecticut 06514

Printed in the United States of America

To the memory of
Margaret W. Farrand

Contents

	List of Illustrations	ix
I.	Strong-minded Women	1
II.	Woman's Profession—Catharine E. Beecher	11
III.	Beware of Sister Jane—Jane G. Swisshelm	56
IV.	The *Lily* and the Bloomer—Amelia Bloomer	107
V.	Greenwood Leaves—"Grace Greenwood" (Sara J. C. Lippincott)	143
VI.	Altogether Doric—Louisa S. McCord	179
VII.	Dusting Mirrors—L. Maria Child	215

Brief preliminary sketches of Catharine Beecher, Amelia Bloomer, and Jane Swisshelm have appeared in the *Delphian Quarterly*, to whose editor I am indebted for permission to reprint several paragraphs here.

Illustrations

Balloon view of Washington   *Frontispiece*

Strong-minded woman cartoon   5

Catharine E. Beecher   *facing page*   11

Title page, *American Woman's Home*   42

Beecher house in Litchfield, from Lyman Beecher's *Autobiography*   55

Jane G. Swisshelm   *facing page*   56
     Courtesy of the Historical Society of Western
      Pennsylvania

Ward in a Union Hospital   97

St. Cloud Visiter   106
     Courtesy of the Minnesota Historical Society

Amelia Bloomer   *facing page*   107
     Courtesy of the Princeton University Library

Bloomer cartoon   129

Grace Greenwood   *facing page*   143

Great Central Fair   167

The Little Pilgrim   178

Louisa S. McCord   *facing page*   179
     Courtesy of the South Caroliniana Library, Uni-
      versity of South Carolina

Cheves McCord   *facing page*   192
     Courtesy of the South Caroliniana Library, Uni-
      versity of South Carolina

South Carolina College   214
L. Maria Child   *facing page* 215
Contrabands coming into camp   250
"Industry Conquers Everything," from the
    Juvenile Miscellany, September, 1826   253

Strong-minded Women

STRONG-MINDED WOMAN used to be a term of reproach. It rings differently today; we hear it as synonymous with pioneer. For we begin to realize that not all the pioneer mothers traveled towards the West in covered wagons. There were wolves and redskins along the narrow trails leading to the editorial office, the hospital, the lecture platform. The strong-minded women broke those trails not, as their shortsighted contemporaries believed, because they were foolish or restless under the duties of their domestic round but because they thought the world could be made better and they wanted to lend a hand.

The second quarter of the nineteenth century was one of the exciting moments in history, especially for a citizen of the United States. In that brave high period it was clear to most Americans that the world was on an upward path of progress. Mankind was perfectible. The millennium could be fixed to a day. Opportunities to help in bringing in the glorious time waited in rows for any man who wanted them, but when a woman started towards the fields she found her way blocked by thorny hedges.

She could not work for any good cause, she discovered, without becoming "unwomanly," without stepping out of "woman's sphere." She could not fight injustice because she was forbidden to study law. She could not plead from the lecture platform for temperance or the freedom of the slave because St. Paul had said that women must keep silence in the churches. Of course then she could not preach. She could not travel about the country to minister to the inmates of prisons and hospitals and asylums unless she were properly escorted. She could not cure the sick for she was forbidden to study medicine. She could not get the intellectual training that she knew was needed for reform work of any kind for her education was confined to the bare elements of grammar and arithmetic, trimmed with a few arts and elegant accomplishments. If she wrote it must be under a pseudonym, preferably masculine, and that she might edit a magazine or newspaper did not occur to anyone. A woman was not even a legal entity; she did not control her own earnings, have the guardianship of her own children, cast her own vote. The woman who wanted to help the world found that she must fight it first.

So she moved, though slowly, towards the cause of woman's rights. She was not, with a few exceptions like Lucy Stone and Elizabeth Cady Stanton, interested in freedom for woman so much as in freedom for mankind, freedom from slavery and pain and fear. Elizabeth Blackwell struggled through poverty, obloquy, and isolation to achieve the first M.D. ever granted to a woman not because she wanted to study medicine—she disliked it during her early years as a student—but because she thought it would be a benefit to women to have physicians of their own sex. Amelia Bloomer put on trousers so that she could do her housework more efficiently and have time to devote to the temperance cause. Catharine Beecher made herself an expert on drainage and ventilation because she realized their importance in the "healthful Christian home." Angelina Grimké steeled herself to address the Massachusetts Legislature because she felt it imperative to tell what she knew of slavery.

This concern for the welfare of humanity, this forgetfulness of self, made the female reformer, caricaturists to the contrary, mild, gentle, and long suffering. She cherished no animosity against her persecutors but genuinely forgave them. She accepted defeat without despair, collected the remnants of her forces, and went on. It was this persistency which seems chiefly to have annoyed her contemporaries. There was no way to stop the creature. Abuse and ridicule proved equally ineffective.

Neither the abuse nor the ridicule was very accurate in its aim. Few of the attackers and the caricaturists seem ever to have looked at a strong-minded woman, much less talked with one. It was only in highly imaginative fiction that the reformer's husband had to mind the baby or the lady novelist burned the mutton chops. The actual strong-minded females were model housekeepers, turning their keen intellects to the planning of balanced meals, the stitching of neat seams, and the clever training of happy children. They declined to believe that domestic customs were immutable and were perpetually devising efficiencies and short cuts which they set down in Frugal Housewives and Domestic Receipt Books to the gratitude of their less imaginative sisters. They neither despised nor neglected the homely round; they simply smoothed it so that they could employ their energies not for their families alone but for mankind.

The strong-minded women made things difficult for the lampoonists also by declining to conform to a type. Strong-mindedness was the product of individual integrity, and though the reformers labored for the same great causes, they worked each in her peculiar way. The patterns of their lives, too, were different, though there are certain similarities of outline.

The geographic background is likely to be New England or the one-generation remove from New England to New York, Pennsylvania, or Ohio. Not until after the Civil War was the term strong-minded heard below the Mason-Dixon Line. The rare Southern woman who, in the 'forties and 'fifties, thought slavery a sin, was constrained, like Mattie Griffith and the Grimké sisters, to migrate to the North. One might make a case for the influence of climate. The social mores of each region certainly played their part; so did education and religion. The Quakers and the Calvinists both believed deeply that they were their brothers' keepers. And the Quaker women were already halfway out of woman's sphere. Their logical sect recognized no distinction between the spiritual abilities of the sexes. Accustomed to speak freely in meeting, the Quaker women were invaluable to the early temperance and suffrage conventions because they were serenely at ease on public platforms. The Calvinists fixed in their daughters for life a tender conscience and a sense of social responsibility even though a courageous and innovating mind might repudiate some of the tenets of the church in which it had been nurtured. At times the religious transition was simply to a freer, more personal interpretation of the scriptures; at others there was transference of allegiance to the Unitarian Church or to the Episcopalian whose clergy seemed to preach a more loving God. Rarely did the strong-minded woman become an atheist, despite the admiration most of them felt for the brilliant Fanny Wright. Her portrait stands as frontispiece to the

The strong-minded woman as her opponents saw her: *Harper's Weekly*, June 11, 1859, "The Orator of the Day Denouncing the Lords of Creation"

three great volumes in which Mrs. Stanton, Miss Anthony, and Mrs. Gage compiled the History of Woman's Suffrage, but the editors, quietly ignoring atheism and free love, write of her as they do of Mary Wollstonecraft and Margaret Fuller, as a pioneer of pioneers, a formulator of the principles by which more and more women were coming to guide their lives.

How revolutionary those lives were, how many barriers there were to be broken, one can sense by studying the points beyond which the strong-minded women refused to go. Sometimes they halted at a restriction which seemed to them set up by Providence, not man; sometimes they thought a particular issue not worth the struggle; sometimes it was simply an instinctive drawing back for which they blamed themselves.

Elizabeth Blackwell, for instance, thought that "it wouldn't be ladylike" to march in the commencement procession with her fellow students when she received her historic medical degree; she entered the church with her brother and sat in a side aisle. Jane Swisshelm drew the line at bloomers: "We would not subject ourself to the rude gaze of a mob on the street, or the insolence of ruffians and boys, for anything less than the salvation of a soul. No dress could be comfortable and convenient to us which would gather half-a-dozen boys to stare at us." Grace Greenwood publicly denied a report that she had gone to the polls in New York City: "That is something I never did, here or elsewhere, and never intend to do till men in power are manly and magnanimous enough to invite me." She was distressed, too, though she felt her own inconsistency, at the sight of women performing in a circus:

By far the most accomplished performers that night were women, in especial two blondes, who did the most daring and astonishing things on the trapeze, and on the tapis, as acrobats, and, O heavens, as tumblers! It was, to me, very dreadful,—a revolting, almost ghastly exhibition of woman's rights. An old-fashioned conservative could not have been more shocked when Elizabeth Blackwell went into medicine, and Antoinette Brown into divinity, than I was at seeing these women, in horrible undress, swinging, and tumbling, and plunging heels over head out of their sphere.

Yet varied as were their points of arrest, individual and idiosyncratic as they themselves might be, the strong-minded women valiantly and effectively held up one another's hands. Though the odds against her might be enormous the pioneer seldom felt herself alone. When she pushed her way through the barbed fence of custom and strode out of her sphere—that sphere, as Caroline Kirkland put it, with "a pudding and a shirt for its two poles"—she immediately encountered friends. If she ventured onto the lecture platform, she found intrepid hostesses who would entertain her in almost any strange city to which she might journey. If she wanted to publicize her cause by organizing a convention, fellow enthusiasts stepped to her side. If she edited a journal, letters and contributions flowed in and sister editors were eager to exchange with her. "It is so like the dropping in of a friend to take tea and spend the evening," wrote the lady editor of the Brattleboro *Democrat*, "when our husband empties his capacious pockets and we find Mrs. Swisshelm [Pittsburgh *Saturday Visiter*], Mrs. Peirson [Lancaster *Literary Gazette*] and Mrs. Bloomer [*The Lily*] beside us, each with a heart full of stirring thoughts." And after 1855 the pioneer had the support of Margaret Fuller's stalwart *Woman in the Nineteenth Century*, the first fine native weapon put into the reformers' hands, a weapon keener, better tempered to their use even than Mary Wollstonecraft's *Vindication of the Rights of Women.*

Most of the strong-minded women also could count their husbands as enthusiastic fellow workers. Strong-minded marriage was a cooperative affair, as Amelia Bloomer took pleasure in explaining through the columns of her journal when a neighbor urged Mr. Bloomer to "exercise his authority" to prevent her from wearing the "short dress." The cooperative husband was quite ready to omit "obey" from the marriage service; to let his wife call herself Lucy Stone instead of Mrs. Henry Blackwell; to regard the money she earned as hers to spend as she pleased. He gallantly faced the dilemma, vividly described by Mrs. Stanton, imposed upon one who escorted "a bloomer":

People would stare; some men and women make rude remarks; boys follow in crowds, or shout from behind fences, so that the gentleman in attendance felt it his duty to resent the insult by showing fight, unless he had sufficient self-control to pursue the even tenor of his way without taking the slightest notice of the commotion his companion was creating.

The strong-minded husband presided at conventions in which his wife was interested, spoke for her causes, wrote articles for her journal. Often it was he who launched her on her strong-minded career by taking her into partnership as the editor of a magazine or making her his professional deputy when he was ill. And he seldom had occasion to regret his twentieth-century attitude; his house was better kept and his children better brought up than most men's.

It becomes apparent, the more one knows her, that the strong-minded woman was a power in her time. She moved in advance of it but not out of sight; looking over her shoulder, she urged her sisters to follow. Any strong-minded biography, therefore, is likely to be illuminating as well as interesting and exciting.

A few of these histories have been set down. Of the scores of others that should be told, most insistent are the stories of the female propagandists, partly because their lives were full of adventure, partly because we have so much of the record in their own words. The practitioners of female persuasion endured perpetual ridicule; they faced ostracism, social and professional; at times they walked in actual peril of their lives; and they wrote of those experiences as well as about their plans for a better world. Catharine Beecher outlined her own "Mental History" to show how character can be influenced by education. Jane Swisshelm set down the varied experiences of *Half a Century* of abolitionist propaganda. Amelia Bloomer explained to the *Lily's* subscribers how she managed to edit a paper while she was running a home. Grace Greenwood described the experiences of an "emancipated female" traveling in Europe and the West. There is much inadvertent autobiography also between the lines of their books and lectures and editorials.

As propaganda, too, their writing is interesting, though not many of them produced distinguished work. They wrote with competence and they knew how to influence their contemporaries. Some of them, like Grace Greenwood and Maria Child, had enjoyed repute as poets or novelists before they turned their skill to the freeing of the slave and the winning of the ballot. Others made their literary names in connection with temperance or abolition or the suffrage cause.

Five of the six women whose stories are told in this book were once well known in the land. Many Americans spoke their names with respect; many more, with laughter or execration but, chiefly because the battles they fought are won, those names today wake only faint echoes in our minds. Five of them—Louisa McCord represents the opposition—fought vigorously for the important causes of their time: abolition, temperance, women's education, women's rights, the improvement of public health, prison reform, and the dress reform which Gerritt Smith thought fundamental to all other feminine freedoms. They helped, some of them, to bring on the Civil War, and they helped to fight it. They took active part in the settling of the West, believing that the new land, taken clean from the hand of God, might be made into a real earthly paradise, filled with cities built straight and tall without room for poverty or crime. The possibilities in each fresh start were infinite and exciting. Blithely, therefore, they confronted danger, discomfort, and hard labor, and they encouraged others to the task, writing effective propaganda for Wisconsin, Minnesota, Iowa, or Colorado.

In all senses of the word the strong-minded woman was a pioneer, concerned perpetually with the future of this country, responsible for its possession of many of those characteristics we most like to call American.

Catharine E. Beecher in 1870

Woman's Profession

CATHARINE E. BEECHER

G OD forgive Christopher Columbus for discovering
such a country," cried a distinguished German
theologian in the year 1836 when he learned that an
American woman had written an able refutation of Jonathan Edwards on the Will. The good gentleman might
have felt less alarm for the future of our United States
had his informant gone on to tell him that the intellectual
Amazon wrote her essay on Fatalism and Free Agency to
console herself for the tragic death of a lover, and that
she devoted the remainder of her life to the education of
her sex for the better performance of their domestic
duties.

Theology and domestic science were related subjects
in the mind of Catharine Esther Beecher—that was the
Amazon's name. She believed that the Creator had appointed woman to a threefold task: the conduct of the
household, the care of the sick, the education of the
young. Housekeeping she saw as a high and honorable
profession and she thought the proper training of its
practitioners a matter of national concern.

Are not the most responsible of all duties committed to the
care of woman? Is it not her profession to take care of mind,
body and soul? And that, too, at the most critical of all periods

of existence? And is it not as much a matter of public concern, that she should be properly qualified for her duties, as that ministers, lawyers, and physicians, should be prepared for theirs?

To Catharine Beecher's contemporaries this was a new gospel, announcing the glad tidings that drudgery might be swallowed up in dignity.

Catharine was born September 6, 1800, the eldest of the eleven children of Lyman Beecher who was said to be the father of more brains than any man in America. Of these Catharine had her full share though the spectacular accomplishments of a younger brother and sister have fixed the names of Henry Ward Beecher and Harriet Beecher Stowe more conspicuously in the national memory.

"Thou little immortal!" young Parson Beecher cried when Grandma Foote put the baby Catharine in his arms. That was typical of his attitude towards his children; he sometimes forgot just how many of them there were who needed dinner but he never ceased to agonize over their souls. At the time of Catharine's birth he was pastor of the Presbyterian church in the little village of Easthampton, Long Island, just at the outset of his energetic career, vigorously practicing the rhetoric and the soul-saving wiles which were to make him a national figure if not quite nationally admired.

To many of his generation Lyman Beecher was a great man; to many of ours he does not seem so, but certainly it must be counted to him as virtue that Roxana Foote loved and married him. Shy, lovely, strong Roxana must always be taken into account when one tries to understand the talents and the mainsprings of that tumultuous group

whose contemporaries regarded them as a race apart—
"saints, sinners and Beechers." The small number of Roxana Foote's letters preserved for us in Lyman Beecher's
Autobiography are chiefly concerned with the state of her
soul and might have been written by any contemporary
Calvinist; there is no individuality, but from the reminiscences of her literary children she rises as a definite and
charming person, sweet tempered, sympathetic, serene,
performing with exquisite craftsmanship any work to
which she set her hand, perpetually curious and studious,
finding life richer and wider than it appeared to most of
her neighbors.

Lyman Beecher as a parent was somewhat less successful. His vitality, enthusiasm, and loud mirth were com-
plementary to a callousness which bordered on brutality.
His younger children, Henry Ward especially, suffered
often, after their mother died, from loneliness and fear,
but Catharine from babyhood was treated by her father
as a companion and the enthusiastic affection with which
she writes of him is palpably genuine. This, for instance,
when she was twenty-five, in a letter to her brother Edward: "There is nothing makes me feel so happy as to
be with him, and nothing so stimulates my intellect as
his conversation."

Catharine shared her father's energy and his rugged
health; she was not troubled by his discipline. In simple
admiration she set down in the reminiscences which she
contributed to his *Autobiography* the statement that

With most of his children, when quite young, he had one,
two, or three seasons in which he taught them that obedience
must be exact, prompt, and cheerful, and by a discipline so
severe that it was thoroughly remembered and feared. Ever

after, a decided word of command was all-sufficient. . . . This method secured such habits of prompt, unquestioning, uncomplaining obedience as made few occasions for discipline. I can remember but one in my own case, . . . This strong and decided government was always attended with overflowing sympathy and love. His chief daily recreations were frolics with his children. I remember him more as a playmate than in any other character during my childhood.

Besides enjoying their company Lyman Beecher had another quality which bound his daughters to him and accounts, perhaps, for the not too easily explained fondness of Roxana. "He had," said Catharine, and she underlined it, "the *gift of expression*. He not only discovered and appreciated all that was good in character and conduct, but he made known his pleased approval." There is no spell which enthralls the female sex like expressed appreciation.

Some of Roxana Beecher's charm her eldest daughter inherited though nothing of her shyness or her delicacy. Buoyant self-confidence was always apparent in the carriage of Catharine's stout frame and the cut of her strong features. "Not handsome," her stepmother said of her, "yet there is hardly anyone who appears better." She was, too, the merriest of girls, all the Beecher energy, which would one day generate reform, expending itself for the present in enjoyment. "A constant stream of mirthfulness" her existence seemed to her often melancholy sister Harriet, who comments wistfully, too, upon her "perfect health."

When she was about nine years old Catharine's horizons of happiness were widened by her father's removal to Litchfield, Connecticut. Lyman Beecher's reputation was growing and Easthampton had begun to seem to him a little narrow. It was difficult, too, to support on $400 a year a wife and five children—Catharine, William, Edward, Mary, George. He did not hesitate long when a call from Litchfield offered him a broader field of usefulness, $800 a year, and his firewood.

Much of its aspect in 1810 remains in the Litchfield of today. The white New England town is set pleasantly in the hills north of New Haven, its meetinghouse facing the village green, its wide streets lined with elms. To the young Beechers the village offered all the proper delights of a New England childhood, skating parties, woodland "rambles," and intellectual adventures. Two important schools embellished the community: Judge Tapping Reeve's Law School, the first established in the United States, and Miss Pierce's Seminary to which young ladies were sent from as far west as Ohio. Dr. Beecher acted as religious adviser to Miss Pierce and her pupils, and his daughters, therefore, were invited to attend the school without payment of fee. In addition to the Law School and Seminary faculties Litchfield counted among its residents learned physicians, senators, and members of congress; it was a community in which good talk was valued, the right sort of community for a teacher to grow up in.

Catharine, when she went to live in Litchfield, had no thought of any occupation so serious as teaching. She concerned herself as little as possible with the more sober aspects of Miss Pierce's Seminary. Her quick wit and glib tongue, practiced in the theological discussions around the family dinner table, gave her teachers the impression that she knew far more than she did. She slid smoothly through her lessons with very little labor, as she cheerfully con-

fessed in later life. The "Mental History," which she included in the preface to her *Common Sense Applied to
Religion,* describes her schoolgirl mind as

a singular compound of the practical and the imaginative.
In youth I had no love for study or for reading even, except-
ing works of the imagination. Don Quixote, the novel to
which I first had access, was nearly committed to memory,
as were a few other novels found at my grandmother's. The
poets, both ancient and modern, were always in reach and
with these materials I early formed a habit of reverie and
castle-building as my chief internal source of enjoyment.
With this was combined incessant activity in practical
matters, such as, at first, doll-dressing and baby-house building; afterward drawing, painting, exploits of merriment,
practical jokes, snow castles and forts, summer excursions,
school and family drama-acting and the like. . . .
Socially, I was good natured and sympathizing, so that
my jokes and tricks were never such as to tease or annoy
others.
Morally, I had a strong sense of justice, but was not naturally so conscientious as some of the other children. Add to
these, persevering energy, great self-reliance, and such cheerful hopefulness that the idea of danger or failure never entered
my head. Even to this day, perfect success and no mischances
are always anticipated till reason corrects the calculation.

Catharine was, in short, what in modern parlance is called
"a leader." Her teachers expressed it, perhaps more accurately, by saying that she was "the busiest of all creatures in doing nothing."
Her circle admired all her talents but respected her most
highly as a poetess. Much of her verse was "of a sprightly
and humorous turn" but some of it was serious enough
for the *Christian Spectator* and her legends of the local

Bantam Indians were ranked with those of John Brace, Miss Pierce's assistant principal.

In 1816 Roxana Beecher died, swiftly, of consumption, and the Beecher household was never so pleasant a place again. "Kind, anxious, economical" Aunt Esther, Dr. Beecher's maiden sister, bravely abandoned the quiet routine of caring for her aged mother and undertook the management of the turbulent parsonage. Though accomplished in the other domestic arts, she was hopelessly clumsy with a needle and the prospect of preparing wardrobes for eight children rose before her as a mountain of difficulty.

It was here [wrote Catharine] that father's good sense, quick discernment, and tender sympathy wisely intervened. He gently and tenderly made me understand the great kindness of grandma and Aunt Esther in giving up their own quiet and comfort to take care of us; he awakened my sympathy for Aunt Esther in her new and difficult position; he stimulated my generous ambition to supply my mother's place in the care of the younger children, especially in the department in which he assured me he knew I would excel, and that was where Aunt Esther most needed help.

Happily, our mother's skill in household handicraft was bequeathed in some good measure to her daughters; and thus stimulated, I, for the first time, undertook all the labor of cutting, fitting, and making all the clothing of the children, as well as my own.

Like most born teachers Catharine liked to learn and under Aunt Esther's tutelage she acquired not only culinary skill but habits of neatness and economy in which she took a histrionic delight since they were foreign to her natural bent. With equal cheerfulness and adaptability she received instruction from the stepmother whom, a year after Roxana's death, Dr. Beecher brought home to his brood. The second Mrs. Beecher, an elegant and pious lady, had been accustomed to "a superior style of house-keeping," the elements of which Catharine swiftly assimilated.

By the time she was twenty Catharine began to feel that she ought to be not only helping with the housework but contributing to the family income. She set herself at last to serious study, working at drawing, painting, and the piano to such good purpose that within a year she had equipped herself to teach those accomplishments and had secured a position in a New London school.

It was during this first year of teaching that Catharine made the acquaintance of Alexander Metcalf Fisher, a brilliant young mathematician and "natural philosopher" just launched upon a professorship and what promised to be a distinguished career at Yale. Harriet, in the biography of her sister which she wrote for *Our Famous Women*, tells, probably adding a few novelist's improvements, a pretty story of their meeting. The young mathematician, who was likewise a poet, was charmed by the verses which a certain "C.D.D." was publishing in the *Christian Spectator*. (Dr. Beecher signed his contributions to the *Spectator* "D.D." so Catharine treated "D.D." as her last name.) Professor Fisher penetrated the disguise, manoeuvred an introduction, and promptly fell in love. So did Catharine. Friends and family thought the match "ideal" and an engagement was soon arranged, the marriage to take place in the spring of 1823 after Professor Fisher's return from Europe. Yale was granting him a year's leave to study teaching methods in French and English universities.

It must have been while she planned her life as Mrs. Alexander Fisher that Catharine evolved her theory of the divinely appointed function of woman, that theory which was to become the foundation of her educational schemes. High spirited, keen minded, aware that she was quite as capable as any of her brothers of dealing with the intricacies of contemporary theology, quite as capable as they of writing and exhortation, having demonstrated fairly that she could earn her own living, Catharine must have argued at length with herself, her lover, and her father too, the right application of her talents. Were the kitchen and the nursery her proper sphere? She liked the exercise of domestic skills and she was very much in love but did she want to commit herself to the years of drudgery and ill-health which marriage seemed to mean to so many of her contemporaries? But need homemaking be drudgery? Was that the Lord's intention? Suppose, in addition to learning the necessary manual skills, one put one's mind to the study of health and diet, of home construction and decoration, of household management, of the education and training of children; suppose one approached housework as a profession, woman's profession? The conviction with which Catharine Beecher in later years preached that evangel suggests that it was the creation not only of her mind but of her heart.

On April 1, 1822 Alexander Fisher sailed for England on the *Albion*. "He has the prospect," wrote Catharine to her friend Louisa Wait, "of a most profitable and delightful time—he has recommendations to all the Universities in England and Scotland, and to most of the great scientific characters there and in France. . . . How much he will have to tell me, and how happy we shall be when we meet again!" In June came word that the *Albion* with all her passengers had gone down in a storm off the Irish coast.

Catharine's grief was intensified by a terrible fear: what of Alexander Fisher's immortal soul? Bright, upright, and useful as his life had been, he had never experienced the essential process of conversion. Unless, by divine grace, that conversion had occurred during his last moments in the tempest his soul was damned to hell. This Catharine was constrained to believe. Lyman Beecher, wracked with misery for her grief, poured out letters of affectionate exhortation or talked with her by the hour in his study but he could not alter his theological principles; he could only hold out the slender permitted hope and entreat his daughter to use this sorrow for the salvation of her own soul. From Edward, the brother three years younger, who was always closest to her in affection, perhaps because he had the best of all the family minds, Catharine derived most comfort. "From the time that I disclosed to you my trifling troubles," he wrote, "I found in you so much kindness and affection . . . that now in your sorrow should I joy to comfort you." And he affirmed his belief that Fisher was not lost, a conviction which he matured into a curious theological scheme, based on the reincarnation of souls and published, years later, as *Conflict of Ages*.

Catharine's love for Alexander Fisher and her admiration for his character were immensely strengthened by a long visit which she made shortly after his death to his parents' farm in Franklin, Massachusetts. There she had opportunity to go over his papers, to read his private journal, to talk day after day with the brother and sisters who had been devoted to him. She became convinced anew that no young manhood could have been more pleasing to God, yet his journal expressly stated that he had been unable to experience "conversion." Sometimes the thought of his eternal misery was more than her mind could bear and she plunged into deep periods of melancholy, but she never gave way completely to despair. Steadying her mind by studying mathematics and tutoring Alexander's sisters, she came at last to a working conclusion: that "there must be a dreadful mistake somewhere" in the theological system in which she had been nurtured, and that until her mind could come to the root of this error she would live as though she believed her father's creed, assuming a virtue that she had not.

Having made this working agreement with her soul Catharine turned to the rebuilding of her material life. Teaching was almost the only occupation open to an unmarried woman and Catharine knew that she could teach but, looking ahead, she hesitated. The schoolroom could be as restricted an orbit as the kitchen.

There seems to be [she wrote to her father, February 15, 1823] no very extensive sphere of usefulness for a single woman but that which can be found in the limits of the schoolroom; but there have been instances in which women of superior mind and acquirements have risen to a more enlarged and comprehensive boundary of exertion, and by their talents and influence have accomplished what, in a more circumscribed sphere of action, would have been impossible. . . .

When I was in Hartford Mr. Hawes lamented the want of a good female school. This and your advice have led me to wish to commence one there.

I might take the general superintendence, and have considerable time for improvement, and also secure the benefit of Edward's assistance while he retains his school there.

Dr. Beecher went to Hartford, made extensive inquiries, and satisfied himself that such a school as Catharine suggested was greatly needed.

It will not, however [he wrote her], answer for you to engage in it listlessly, expecting yourself to superintend and do a little, and have the weight of the school come on others. I should be ashamed to have you open, and keep only a commonplace, middling sort of school. It is expected to be of a high order; and, unless you are willing to put your talents and strength into it, it would be best not to begin.

Listlessness was not in Catharine's nature. The insistence of something practical to be done was just what her spirits needed. She set vigorously to work and by the end of April the Hartford papers were announcing:

Misses C. and M. Beecher will open in this place a School intended exclusively for those who wish to pursue the higher branches of female education. It is hoped that those who attend, will feel disposed to acquire a thorough knowledge of the most necessary parts of education, such as Geography, Grammar, Rhetoric, etc., and will afterward advance to a higher and more extended knowledge of science and literature. None will be admitted under the age of 12, unless unusually advanced in their education. Terms for tuition, $6 per quarter. Lessons will be given in Music at $10 per quarter, and in drawing at $2 per quarter. The term will commence May 20, 1823.

The school began with seven pupils reciting in a room over a harness store on Main Street. It grew so rapidly that it had to seek new quarters twice within three years.

By 1826 eighty girls were receiving instruction in a large room in the basement of a church. Then a boarding department was added and two more teachers. Little Harriet, who had come on to Hartford as a pupil, developed into a highly successful teacher of composition. Mary, the Miss M. of the original partnership, married and retired into private life, the only Beecher who ever did so. In the eyes of Hartford parents Miss Beecher was conducting an institution of a "higher order" but Miss Beecher herself was not so sure. While she organized and taught and studied Latin with her brother Edward she imagined the perfect school and began to systematize that ideal of female education it was to be her lifework to promulgate. In 1827 she published her first piece of propaganda, an article on "Female Education" which the *American Journal of Education* printed with admiring comment.

Miss Beecher's chief concern in this essay was to persuade parents that the education of daughters ought to be taken seriously and to persuade the community that "refined and well educated" women confer a "beneficial influence" on society. Then she proposed, in the usual practice of female schools, alterations which the *Journal* approved but which seemed to a good many Hartford fathers foolishly new fangled.

She wished, for instance, that her pupils should enter and leave school at stated times of year, not at the whim and convenience of each set of parents. She wanted to break down the prevalent notion that a school was excellent in proportion to the number of subjects in which it offered instruction. She wanted her teachers to be specialists, teaching only one or two subjects in which they were really well versed. She wanted separate rooms for each class to recite in; not one great hall where everything went on at once. She advocated a new form of exercise called, "from the Greek," calisthenics. She wanted "apparatus" for her school: blackboards, maps, charts, even a magic lantern. She believed that information learned by rote was not the true measure of an education; she wanted her pupils to understand and be able to discuss the information they absorbed.

A school of the kind Miss Beecher visualized could never be a money-making institution; it must be, she was sure, endowed by the community. She asked Hartford for $5,000 and, when the fathers of the community demurred, she went to their wives, and got it. "This was my first experience," she wrote in her *Educational Reminiscences*, "of the moral power and good judgment of American women, which has been my chief reliance ever since."

For four years the Hartford Female Seminary flourished, the happiness and progress of its young ladies indicating that perhaps Miss Beecher's educational innovations were sound after all. Catharine worked indefatigably, teaching, organizing, planning, making textbooks when she could find none to her liking, one in arithmetic, one in Mental and Moral Philosophy. She wrote a little poetry, too, now and then, publishing it in the Connecticut *Observer*. She was not so full of mirth as she had been at twenty but she was lively in conversation, able to make any party go, thoroughly interested, apparently, in the work she was doing. The "rules of health" which she preached to her young ladies she practiced conscientiously herself, sleeping eight hours, exercising two each day in the open air, usually riding horseback of which she was very fond. Then suddenly, when she was thirty-one, without, by her account, a sign of warning, she went to pieces. "I found the entire fountain of nervous energy exhausted. I could not read a page or write a line, or even listen to conversation without distress." This "utter and irretrievable prostration" she attributed to the fact that, despite her careful regimen, she had never taken time for rest and relaxation. She had been afraid, one supposes, to give herself time to think. She had not yet found the explanation of that "dreadful mistake somewhere," and the only way to live was to keep her mind perpetually occupied with problems on another level.

Fortunately, just at the moment when her too tightly strung nerves gave way, when it became physically impossible for her to carry on the details of school administration, a new and exciting prospect of usefulness opened, commanding her attention. Her father was offered the presidency of Lane Seminary in Cincinnati and heard the call as a summons to the evangelization of the West:

The moral destiny of our nation [he wrote Catharine], and all our institutions and hopes, and the world's hopes, turns on the character of the West, and the competition now is for that of preoccupancy in the education of the rising generation, in which Catholics and infidels have got the start of us. . . . this is not with me a transient flash of feeling, but a feeling as if the great battle is to be fought in the Valley of the Mississippi . . . if I go, it will be part of my plan that *you* go, and another that Edward, and probably all my sons and all my daughters who are willing to go.

Catharine made the exploratory journey to Cincinnati with her father and wrote the family enthusiastic reports of Walnut Hills, on the outskirts of the city, where Lane

Seminary was located. "I never saw a place so capable of being rendered a Paradise by the improvements of taste as the environs of this city. . . . I think a very pleasant society can be selected from the variety which is assembled here." "The folks here are very anxious to have a school on our plan set on foot here." Pious people were hard pressed to educate their children, for the only school for girls was kept by a lady who "writes tragedies for the theatre, and takes her pupils to see them acted."

Catharine did not of course feel strong enough to assume the management of a school herself but she browbeat one of the ablest teachers in her Hartford Seminary into undertaking it. Mary Dutton was reluctant to try an experiment which involved so violent an uprooting but Catharine showed her her duty. When logic failed she could usually hound a soul into the true path by her vigorous persistence.

After the great move had been made and the Beecher life adjusted to its new environment, the household organized, the school under way, when the family began to feel as though they were really Westerners, Catharine, not quite so pressed with hourly care as she had been in Hartford, found, and permitted herself, the leisure to think again on her continual problem. This time she worked it through and with sufficient conviction to put her solution into print. A Beecher might keep doubts to himself but never conclusions.

In 1836 she published *Letters on the Difficulties of Religion*, setting forth her version of the Calvinist revolt so typical of her generation. She had ceased to believe in the inate depravity of man; morality now seemed to her more important than piety, and her God must be a God of love. She had learned much of God's essential nature, she recorded, through her own experience in attempting wisely to govern her Hartford school. Serious religious journals reviewed the *Letters* and the *Biblical Repository* stated admiringly that "we should never have suspected that it proceeded from the hand of a lady." The writer added, however, that if St. Paul were now on earth he would undoubtedly "discourage the female sex, however gifted or learned, from mixing themselves in theological and ecclesiastical controversies."

Three years later Catharine had worked out even more completely her scheme of salvation and she then published, in the *Biblical Respository* (October, 1839), "An Essay on Cause and Effect in Connection with the Doctrine of Fatalism and Free Agency." Authorities, including her theological brother-in-law Calvin Stowe, considered that essay and the *Letters* the ablest refutation yet written of Edwards on the Will.

This new theology of love Harriet put into novel form twenty years later when the awful question of the relative importance of piety and morality was posed for her sharply by the death of a nineteen-year-old son. In *The Minister's Wooing* she fused her sister's spiritual struggle with her own, putting some of Catharine's phrases and the conclusions to which they both had come into the mouth of an intuitively righteous old colored woman: "Honey, darlin', ye a'n't right,—dar's a drefful mistake somewhar . . . Why, de Lord a'n't like what ye tink,— He *loves* ye, honey!"

Though, according to Catharine's own account, it took her twenty years to recover from her Hartford break-down—she was constantly obliged to rest and to restore herself at water cures—the work she performed in her lifetime would seem a considerable accomplishment to anyone except a Beecher. After she had written the *Letters* and the "Essay on Cause and Effect" her mind was freed from its burden of terror and was able to grapple not only with the practical details of life but with the theories behind. She began to formulate her youthful feelings about woman's mission into a systematic theology. God has appointed woman, she announced—the Beechers were always definite concerning the intentions of the Lord—to the noblest of all professions: the care of the home, the sick, and the young. For this woman needs not only the fullest possible education, on a par with her most talented brother's, but also technical training as detailed and elaborate as that of the doctor or lawyer.

"Woman's profession": it was a fine slogan and rallying phrase, and an alarmingly radical concept. Housework in the mid-nineteenth century had fallen into low estate. It was for the most part laborious drudgery, ill performed and ill paid. A lady undertook it only when forced by straightened means. This, Catharine Beecher felt, was all wrong. That "larger usefulness" towards which her mind had turned longingly at twenty-three began to take shape. She would labor to convince her sex of the dignity of the work to which they are called and to persuade the nation of the importance of properly educating its female citizens. Corollary to this was a desire to evangelize the West by schools as her father was evangelizing it from the pulpit.

Her plan of campaign was practical, derived from first-hand knowledge of conditions both East and West. Travel was believed to be the best remedy for her nervous state and though most travel in the 'thirties and 'forties was a physically exhausting affair, Catharine found real refreshment in the absence of responsibility—no school to oversee, no housekeeping—and in the new sights and people for which she had indefatigable appetite. She was never content merely to look at monuments or scenery but went about asking questions and amassing information with all the energy of a twentieth-century journalist. Curious, for example, to learn the effect of factory labor on women, she spent several days in Lowell where she "conversed with agents, overseers, clergymen, physicians, editors, ladies resident in the place, and a large number of the operatives themselves." Her findings, reported in detail, convinced her that factory work was not woman's appointed task. The visit to Lowell was part of a tour of New England taken with her friend Mary Lyon who was raising funds for Mt. Holyoke Seminary. Talking eagerly with everyone she met Catharine was concerned to find how many cultivated women were longing to be of use in the world but quite unable to find a channel for their talents and energies. Then, traveling and visiting in the West, she was appalled at the educational deserts there, commercially thriving communities whose children were growing up in ignorance because there were no teachers among the citizens. The synthesizing of these needs, it seemed to her, would direct many women towards their true profession.

To effect that synthesis Catharine Beecher organized the Board of National Popular Education. Planning and persuasion seemed to her woman's work, but not administration. She sought for her society a masculine executive and finally persuaded an ex-governor of Vermont, William Slade, to serve. To present her plan to the public Catharine prepared an address, *The Evils Suffered by American Women and American Children*. Her brother Thomas, who went on tour with her, read it while she sat beside him on the platform.

She presented her case also in *The Duty of American Women to their Country*, a small book containing both a moving description of the country's educational need and a statement of the plan by which the Board of National Popular Education proposed to meet it. Miss Beecher begins with an account of the horrors of the French Revolution which she ascribes to the lack of popular education. She then describes the absence of education which so distressed her in our Western states, and summons American women to the rescue of their country. It is propaganda of the most effective kind: a stirring emotional appeal followed by concrete suggestions of "what to do about it." The book was read, the address was listened to by many distinguished gatherings, and the funds began to come in. To augment them Miss Beecher offered a percentage on the sales of her *Treatise on Domestic Economy* and her *American Housekeeper's Receipt Book*.

In 1847 the Board of Popular Education began to function. Governor Slade traveled through the West and South, lecturing, organizing local committees, and arranging for the reception of the teachers whom Miss Beecher recruited in the Eastern states. To assist her in the selection of candidates she prepared a form to be filled out by the applicant's clergyman: "Has she energy, decision and perseverance? Is she naturally of a hopeful or despondent disposition? Faults are expected in all, but it must be known what they are in order to calculate for them."

By June thirty-five young teachers were gathered together in Albany, where they were housed by benevolent
ladies of the community while they underwent a month
of special training. Miss Beecher lectured to them on

The best method to pursue in classifying a school made up of
all ages from five to twenty, and of all stages of advancement.
How to meet the difficulty, when half the parents furnish no
books, and of those provided no two books are alike. Simple
and economical methods of securing ventilation, warmth in
winter, and coolness in summer, and various articles of school
furniture and apparatus, when parents think these matters of
little consequence. Methods of training children to neatness,
order, and punctuality, whose parents regard these things as
of no consequence. Methods of training children to be truth-
ful and honest, when all domestic and social influences tend
to weaken such habits. How to use the Bible for imparting
instruction in both moral and spiritual duties, without giving
occasion for sectarian jealousy and alarm. How to preserve a
teacher's health from the risks of climate and the dangers of
overexertion and excessive care. How to secure improvements in diet and domestic comforts in a neighborhood without giving offence. How to teach the laws of health by the aid
of simple drawings on the blackboard, so that children can
copy them on slates to take home and explain to their parents.
How to meet the amiable but troublesome amor patriae,
which is jealous in regard to foreign improvements. How to
teach certain branches of Domestic Economy, so that parents
will be pleased, and willing to adopt improvements.

The young ladies also listened to lectures on teaching
methods by the principal of the Albany Normal School
and received instruction in calisthenics.

The project attracted a good deal of public notice,
most of the press adopting of course the standard anti-

feminist attitude of amusement. Only one thing, said the Cincinnati *Daily Gazette*, "will be likely seriously to interfere with Miss Beecher's plan of supplying good teachers to the whole Mississippi Valley. That, however, may be fatal to the whole scheme; we allude to the rapidity with which the rosy, tidy, industrious and well-educated Yankee girls that come out West, get married here." New England papers echoed the joke but Miss Beecher was unperturbed. Let the teachers marry, she said, and new ones take their places. The good influence will be scattered so much more widely. In preparing her young women to teach she was also preparing them for wifehood. "The school-room is the truest avenue to domestic happiness." By September another group was in training in Hartford.

The Board functioned admirably at first, the West was being evangelized and woman's profession advanced; but before long administrative trouble developed. Miss Beecher's genius was for propaganda, not for administration. She could sway her fellows in the mass by the power of her words and her own inner conviction but she was incapable of the compromise and adjustment necessary for working week after week with individuals.

She could never give a deputy a properly free hand, and disagreement and conflict inevitably arose. It must be admitted, too, that Catharine Beecher was now displaying a good many of the traits 'of the caricaturists' strong-minded woman. At twenty-three, she had accepted spinsterhood and assumed authority with the opening of the Hartford school. The habit of domination had grown. After she attained spiritual certainty, which involved the courage to disagree with her father, there were few mortals whose opinions seemed to her superior to her own.

What resulted was not conceit but an imperturbable self-assurance, admirable as well as amusing, mingled as it was with the qualities which had made her so attractive in youth, that liveliness and "cheerful hopefulness" so strong that the idea of danger or failure never occurred to her. A story her grandnephew tells of her at seventy is probably a good portrait of her character from thirty on.

President Andrew White of Cornell was visited in his office one morning by a vigorous old lady with high-bridged nose and bobbing side curls. She announced that she had just discovered in the Cornell catalogue a course for which she had long been looking and desired to be enrolled. Dr. White politely explained that as yet Cornell had no courses open to women.

"Oh, that is quite all right," Miss Beecher assured him; "in fact I prefer to take it with men."

As no further discussion of the matter seemed possible the president resignedly inquired if he might assist Miss Beecher in finding lodgings in the town. She replied that she proposed to reside in a certain campus dormitory. In some consternation Dr. White informed her that that was a dormitory for young men; there were no campus accommodations for ladies.

"I have inspected the accommodations," answered Miss Beecher, "and find them entirely satisfactory, and as for those young men, who are of appropriate ages to be my grandsons, they will not trouble me in the least."

It is of record that she was exceedingly popular with the young men of appropriate ages to be her grandsons, but one can imagine that Governor Slade may not always have found it easy to work with Miss Beecher.

There were financial difficulties, too, for Catharine

was far more skillful in raising funds than in administering them. She had the typical Beecher attitude towards money. A Beecher seldom wanted money for himself. Harriet and Henry Ward enjoyed the luxuries that came to them with success and national popularity but they, like the rest of the family, made no relation in their minds between the work they did and the recompense they received for it. Schools, pastorates, the writing of books were undertaken not for profit but as service to the Lord. No Beecher reckoned the hours or the strength he expended, only the need for the labor. But they did take it for granted that while they worked for the kingdom the Lord would provide for their fundamental needs. Usually He did. When Lyman Beecher could no longer live on his salary a call sounded to some richer parish, where also there would be more of the Lord's work to do. While the second Mrs. Beecher wept through the night over debts there seemed no possibility of paying, Lyman went calmly to sleep, and next morning would come a knock on the door and an anonymous gift of a hundred dollars, thank-offering from some father whose son Dr. Beecher had converted.

Lyman's sons operated on the same plan. So did Catharine. She asked from her Hartford Seminary only a simple living; the profits she turned back into its improvement. The royalties from most of her books went into the causes she was sponsoring. In return, she expected from the Lord, or his servants, traveling expenses, homes to stay in when she was on a mission, and a living wage. Her friends, trustees, and deputies, therefore, were occasionally subject to financial worry.

The history of the disagreement with Governor Slade

is neither edifying nor interesting. In the end Catharine, at his insistence, withdrew altogether from active connection with the Board. She was bitterly disappointed at her failure to accomplish what she had hoped but she did not make the disagreement public and she did not bear malice. When she had organized another association, with an even broader purpose, she referred to it as an extension of the work of the National Board of Popular Education.

The new organization, the American Women's Educational Association, began to function in 1852. It proposed to establish in important Western cities endowed institutions "to include all that is gained by normal schools, and also to train women to be healthful, intelligent, and successful wives, mothers and house-keepers." When a city could offer land, buildings, and a guaranteed number of pupils the Association agreed to furnish endowment and guidance in the setting up of an institution.

Catharine's propaganda for the new organization was as successful as it had been for the first. One curious indication of its effectiveness is the warning she was constrained to publish that "well-dressed women in various parts of the country" were mulcting the public by posing as her agents. She interested influential ladies in communities East and West and persuaded to service on her Board of Managers women of national reputation: the distinguished teacher Zilpah Grant Banister, Lydia Sigourney, the poetess, and Sarah Josepha Hale of *Godey's Lady's Book*. That able though time-serving editress gave the Association very useful publicity in her magazine.

In Iowa, at Dubuque, and in Illinois, at Quincy, the Association started schools which flourished briefly. In Milwaukee, Wisconsin, they established an institution

which is still actively advancing women's education "at
the West." Milwaukee-Downer College pays honor to
Catharine Beecher as its founder. The Association did
good work also in dinning into the public mind by one
device or another—petitions, meetings, the preparation
of textbooks, the planning of courses of study for schools
—the necessity of training woman for her profession.

Through all the rest of her life Catharine Beecher went
up and down the land acting as an officer of the Women's
Educational Association or promoting in some other way
the honor of woman's profession. At seventy she made a
brief attempt to restore the prestige of the Hartford Seminary, which had fallen on lean days. Then she lectured
for a term on the "Ethics of Home Life" in Dio Lewis'
school in Lexington. His system of physical education was
based on an English plan she had popularized, and he admired her also as rarely gifted in the training of girls for
"the duties of Christian womanhood." At seventy-five
Miss Beecher, living in Brooklyn with her brother Edward, was organizing the Twenty-third Ward Charity,
to encourage economy in the households of the wealthy
and to afford relief to those in distress without counte-
nancing pauperism. In 1877 she moved to the home of her
brother Thomas, in Elmira, New York. A week before
her death of an apoplectic stroke, May 12, 1878, she was
writing of her plans for "an extended tour for the improvement of common school education among the working
classes."

During all this travel and organizing activity she was
turning out book after book and planning others, all of
them concerned, directly or indirectly, with the advancement of Woman's Profession. This seemed to her so clearly

the divine plan for her sex that all other female causes appeared as heresies, and Miss Beecher the reformer became often a serious opponent of reform. She would not even rejoice at the opening of Mt. Holyoke and Vassar because those institutions offered woman no special training for her domestic duties. *The True Remedy for the Wrongs of Women* Catharine Beecher called the statement of her creed which she published in 1851, and that was the burden of her opposition to suffrage and other proposed alleviations of the female state: they were not the true remedy. It is not improved property and marriage laws that woman needs, she said, nor is it the ballot; woman is not called to public office nor to any public labor for the general good; such activity merely deflects energies which the Creator has designed for other uses. In short, the strong-minded Catharine Beecher believed in "woman's sphere." She defined it in the *Essay on Slavery and Abolition* which she addressed, in 1837, to Angelina Grimké:

A woman may seek the aid of cooperation and combination among her own sex, to assist her in her appropriate offices of piety, charity, maternal and domestic duty; but whatever, in any measure, throws woman into the attitude of a combatant, either for herself or others—whatever binds her in a party conflict—whatever obliges her in any way to exert coercive influences, throws her out of her appropriate sphere.

When she opposed a cause, as she did with abolition or woman's suffrage, Catharine Beecher did it without belligerency, in the spirit of Christian controversy.

As in the physical universe the nicely balanced *centripetal* and *centrifugal* forces hold in steady curve every brilliant orbit, so, in the moral world, the radical element, which would forsake the beaten path of ages, is held in safe and steady course by the conservative; while that, also, is preserved from dangerous torpor by the antagonistic power. And so, while claiming to represent the conservative element, I meet with respect and kindness my centrifugal friend.

Thus she introduced the case for the opposition at a woman's suffrage convention in New York, presided over, piquantly enough, by her brother Henry Ward.

But more than argument Catharine Beecher enjoyed preaching, addressing in print the largest audience she could command. She wrote constantly on domestic science, on religion, on education, mingling them in her titles as she related them in her thoughts.

Only one of her publishing ventures proved unfortunate: her collaboration with President William Holmes McGuffey of Cincinnati College in the editing of his fourth *Eclectic Reader*. The rules for posture, emphasis, and pronunciation in that *Reader* were prepared, he announced in his preface, with the assistance of "a very distinguished Teacher, whose judgment and zeal in promoting the cause of education have often been commended by the American people."

The very distinguished teacher's zeal seems, in this instance, to have outrun her judgment. She worked on the *Reader* in such haste that she sometimes found it more convenient to borrow a rule from another book than to compose one and the publisher of *Worcester's Reader* brought suit for plagiarism. Miss Beecher fought the charge and, since it was difficult to determine just who had borrowed from whom, the matter was settled out of court. More to the collaborator's credit are the two pieces which she composed for the *Reader*, comparative character studies of "Henry Martyn and Lord Byron" and of "Chesterfield and Paul."

Once sure of her own spiritual convictions Catharine Beecher became concerned to devise a system of religious education for children which should lead them naturally to the love of God, sparing them such miseries as she had experienced. *Common Sense Applied to Religion*, which she published in 1857, is an elaboration of the textbook on Mental and Moral Philosophy prepared when she was at the Hartford Seminary and considered then too un-orthodox for print. In 1860 came *An Appeal to the People in Behalf of their Rights as Authorized Interpreters of the Bible;* in 1864, *Religious Training of Children in the School, the Family and the Church*, in which she publicly rejected the "soul-withering system" of Presbyterianism and announced her adherence to the Episcopal Church, with which her sister Harriet had also affiliated.

These books were welcome guides to the woman who was trying to carry on in a professional spirit the duties of homemaking and child training but even more wel-come was the *Treatise on Domestic Economy for the Use of Young Ladies at Home and at School* which Miss Beecher published in 1841.

The *Treatise on Domestic Economy* is Catharine Beecher's most important accomplishment. Twentieth-century teachers of domestic science refer to it with re-spect as a classic, the pioneer volume in the field. Catharine Beecher treated housekeeping as a science and women who had practiced it all their lives were delighted to find that they had been speaking prose.

The *Treatise* was followed, in 1842, by a *Domestic Receipt Book* which presented its receipts in language "short, simple, and perspicuous" and guaranteed that they had all been tested by "superior housekeepers." The plan and purpose of the book as described in its preface is a fine example of the Beecher ability to combine realism and the ideal:

To present a good supply of the rich and elegant dishes demanded at such entertainments, and yet to set forth so large and tempting a variety of what is safe, healthful, and good in connection with such warnings and suggestions as it is hoped may avail to promote a more healthful fashion in regard both to entertainments and to daily table supplies. No book of this kind will sell without an adequate supply of the rich articles which custom requires, and in furnishing them the writer has aimed to follow the example of Providence, which scatters profusely both good and ill, and combines therewith the caution alike of experience, revelation, and conscience, "choose ye that which is good, that ye and your seed may live."

The demand for both books was enormous. A new edition of the *Treatise*, "revised with additions," was brought out in 1842 and in the course of the next thirty years Miss Beecher's principles of domestic economy were offered to an eager public in at least a dozen different forms.

Catharine Beecher's domestic theory had, as we have seen, been carefully thought out and required no alteration, but she never tired of learning and experimenting in its practical applications. She kept up with current developments in chemistry, medicine, mechanical invention, and continually modernized and improved the advice and guidance she offered to her readers. She spread her gospel also with a set of *Letters to Persons Who Are*

Engaged in Domestic Service (1842) and with articles in *Godey's Lady's Book* and *Harper's* under such arresting titles as "Woman's Profession Dishonored," or "The American People Starved and Poisoned."

The most attractive and comprehensive shape which the principles of domestic economy took was *The American Woman's Home*, published in 1869 under the double signature of Catharine E. Beecher and Harriet Beecher Stowe. Mrs. Stowe's contribution was a selection from her *House and Home* papers which had been running successfully in the *Atlantic*. *The American Woman's Home*, "embellished profusely with pictures" and handsomely bound in green and gold, was brought out by J. B. Ford of New York who seems to have weaned Miss Beecher from Harper by assuring her that an illustrated edition of her *Treatise*, with some of the material from the *Receipt Book* included, would sell at least 50,000 copies. It would be even more popular, they said, than her brother-in-law Calvin Stowe's *Origin and History of the Books of the Bible*.

Ford also issued a special school edition of *The American Woman's Home* with exercises and "questions that will promote thought and discussion in class rooms." The original *Treatise* had been included in the Massachusetts School Library and had been used as a textbook by public schools and female seminaries in all sections of the country. The missionary teacher, too, had used it in her civilizing of the West. Miss Beecher's *Educational Reminiscences* quote a letter showing the book in action:

I have read your *Domestic Economy* through to the family, one chapter a day. They like it, and have adopted some of your suggestions in regard to *order* and to *health*. They used

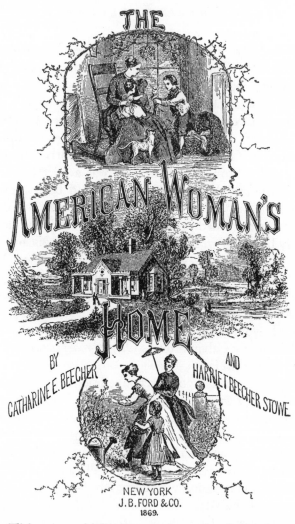

THE

AMERICAN WOMAN'S

HOME

BY CATHARINE E. BEECHER AND HARRIET BEECHER STOWE.

NEW YORK
J.B. FORD & CO.
1869.

Title page of Miss Beecher's textbook for those
practicing "woman's profession"

to drink coffee three times a day. Now they use it only once a day. Their bread used to be heavy and half-baked, but I made yeast by the receipt in your book, and thus made some good bread. They were much pleased with it, and I have made such ever since.

Never was a textbook so crammed with propaganda as *The American Woman's Home*. Seldom has a textbook been such good reading. Catharine was a master of exposition. She could make the instructions for covering an ottoman interesting, the principles of ventilating a kitchen lucid. And she could make both seem important, acts to be performed with care and skill to the greater glory of God. The material, the intellectual, and the spiritual meet and mingle on her pages with that unself-conscious ease which is one of the most engaging traits of the Puritan civilization. "The reason why cells increase must remain a mystery, until we can penetrate the secrets of vital force —probably forever. But the mode in which they multiply is as follows." "The person who decides what shall be the food and drink of a family, and the modes of its preparation, is the one who decides, to a greater or less extent, what shall be the health of that family."

The sections from the pen of Mrs. Stowe—on cookery, on fresh air, on home decoration—are lively and good in their kind but they serve to point up the virtues of Catharine's style. Harriet is the literary lady concerned to say things with a flourish, determined that you shall think not only that her ideas are good but that she was a clever little woman to have had such ideas. Catharine is completely unconcerned with anything except her subject, how to make it clear and prove it true, yet her individuality comes through as sharply as her sister's.

For all its wide range of contents *The American Woman's Home* has a clear continuity. Read it on successive evenings, as the missionary teacher did, a chapter at a time, and you will find taking shape before you a clear plan and picture of an ideal nineteenth-century home. The book is one of the most comprehensive and useful records we have of the way of life of our grandmothers. Even the Glossary "of such words and phrases as may not easily be understood by the young reader" is a treasury of information for the connoisseur of nineteenth-century novels who has puzzled over the social distinction between "in-grain" and "Brussels" carpet or the precise appearance of an astral lamp. To say nothing of Miss Beecher's occasional fine Johnsonian definitions: "*Cosmetics:* Preparations which some people foolishly think will preserve and beautify the skin."

The book is dedicated to the Women of America, "in whose hands rest the real destinies of the republic, as moulded by the early training and preserved amid the maturer influences of home." The text is embellished with diagrams, plans and pictures, many of them certainly the products of Catharine's own pencil, all of them admirably suited to their purpose.

The first chapter presents a picture of the Christian family, whose distinctive feature is "self-sacrificing labor of the stronger and wiser members to raise the weaker and more ignorant to equal advantages." The family state is "the aptest earthly illustration of the heavenly kingdom, and in it woman is its chief minister." Then follows a highly practical plan for the ideal house, designed for economy of building, for warmth, light, and good ventilation, and also for convenient housekeeping, so that a family of normal size can operate it with little or no domestic help. Manual labor played an important role in all Miss Beecher's schemes. She was in the current of the movement which was rising in America at about the time she moved to Cincinnati. That man should work with his hands was, she thought, dignified, beautiful, and part of the divine plan. And woman also. "God made woman so that her health and comfort are best promoted by doing the work she is appointed to perform. The tending of children, the house-work of a family, duly combined with its sedentary pursuits, all tend to strengthen and develop those central muscles of the body that hold its most important organs in their place."

The American Woman's ideal home incorporates a rather surprising number of what we choose to call twentieth-century ideas. It is designed in sections, so that some rooms can be finished later as money becomes available and the family expands. An ingenious rolling screen permits the space which is a bedroom by night to become a sitting room and dressing room by day. The interior woodwork is oiled chestnut or pine, "cheaper, handsomer, and more easy to keep clean than painted wood." Laundry tubs are fitted with spigots and plugs to save the labor of carrying water and emptying. Built-in shelves, cupboards, and boxes within easy reach of the stove contain all materials necessary for cooking. There is even a hinged cover which turns the sink into a worktable and a tumbler tray to facilitate table setting. Closet and bedroom arrangements are equally ingenious.

Instructions for contriving all these devices are complete to the last detail. The pivots of the partition screen, for instance, the housewife is told, should be rubbed with hard soap, then a child can move it easily. Mingled with the carpentry are interesting suggestions for the ordering of family life and the education of the young. The plans call for two conservatories opening out of the living rooms because "every child should cultivate flowers and fruits to sell and to give away, and thus be taught to learn the value of money and to practice both economy and benevolence."

And finally Miss Beecher lets her imagination expand her house into a series. She builds up one of those ideal communities so fascinating to the nineteenth-century American mind. She disapproved most of the communal experiments of her time because they did not operate on the family plan. What she dreamed of was a group of Christian homes situated in "some of the beautiful Southern uplands" where it would be possible to raise fruits and vegetables the year around and where railroads would provide a steady market. There would be a central church, school, library, "hall for sports, and a common laundry, (taking the most trying part of domestic labor from each house)." All the children would be taught to work with their hands as a healthful and honorable duty and the wealth thus economized—for these citizens are to live below their incomes—would go to diffuse similar enjoyments and culture among the ignorant and neglected in more desolate sections of the nation.

Having established the moral tone of her American home Miss Beecher goes on to instruct the housewife in the more difficult technical problems she will be called upon to master, such as the correct ventilation of a room or the management of an elaborate cook stove. The latter subject is introduced with the dry comment that the young woman who gives it her best attention will find her mind expanded and improved quite as much as though she had mastered the first problem in Euclid.

These chapters are all admirably planned and executed teaching. A clear description of how we breathe, how air circulates, and what its chemical components are makes the suggested methods of ventilation seem inevitable, from the window opened a crack at the top to the elaborately diagramed flues and air passages. One is continually impressed by Miss Beecher's knowledge of her subject, so far of course as contemporary knowledge went. The modern reader will smile over the firm statement that "to bathe daily in warm water is seriously debilitating," shiver over the instructions for packing fever patients in wet sheets, and take exception perhaps to some of the dogma on nutrition, but what he deplores will be the state of nineteenth-century medicine, not the state of Catharine Beecher.

The progressive principles of her day Miss Beecher advocated but she did not ride hobbies. Her convictions were based on extended reading, investigation, and experiment. She talked with doctors, engineers, and physics professors; she was acquainted with the most recent experiments in science and medicine. The method of ventilation she advised, for instance, had been used successfully in military hospitals in Washington and in A. T. Stewart's New York hotel for his workers.

To knowledge Miss Beecher added enthusiasm. She wrote passionately of ventilation because she felt that her early ignorance of the subject and the long hours she spent as a young teacher in fetid classrooms had much to do with her nervous collapse. Ignorance, she believed, was responsible for most of the ill-health of American women, and that they should have abundant health was the very foundation of her schemes for their dignity and happiness. How could a housewife practice her high profession lying upon a sofa?

And Mama's sofa was becoming the central object in more and more American homes. The airless dwelling where "modern" stoves had replaced the fireplace, the disabling enormities of fashionable dress, seldom sillier than in the mid-nineteenth century, the growing disinclination to domestic labor as ugly and unladylike, all these were rapidly turning American women into nervous invalids. Catharine Beecher was aware of this from her wide observation and experience but to promulgate her principles she felt the need of supporting facts. She wanted statistics and she contrived an ingenious method for getting them. Perhaps it should not be reckoned to her as virtue but she is one of the first recorded users of the questionnaire.

Her acquaintance among the female sex was large. She had, she calculated, nine married sisters and sisters-in-law, and fourteen married female cousins. The roster of her former pupils was a long one and many of them kept in close touch with her after their schooldays, inviting her to visit them and consulting her on their personal problems. These females and "most of the married ladies whom I met either on my journeys, or at the various health establishments at which I stopped" were asked to further Miss Beecher's research.

Each one made a list, by initials only, of the ten married women she knew best in her community and set down opposite each a general statement of her health: perfectly healthy, well (but not strong), delicate, diseased, invalid. The results gave a picture even more horrifying than Miss Beecher's own impression. In group after group only one or two perfectly healthy women were listed among the ten; often there were none at all. These statistics, changing the initials "as a matter of delicacy," but retaining the names of cities to show that her survey was countrywide, Catharine Beecher published in her *Letters to the People on Health and Happiness*, a small popular textbook of physiology and medicine much of which is condensed into the health chapters in *The American Woman's Home*.

Remedies for this alarming condition of female health Miss Beecher investigated as assiduously as she had collected the statistics. Many current popular treatments she tried herself at firsthand in an attempt to relieve her own nervous debility. (It seems to have taken most of the time a form which would today be called sciatica.) She was no hypochondriac; she did not enjoy being doctored but genuinely wanted to be well. It was her indomitable hopefulness and tireless scientific curiosity which kept her perpetually trying cures. She experimented with "washings," with drugs, with diets, with carbonate of iron, with tartar emetic pustules on the spine(!), but she found no visible relief until she visited a water cure establishment where great stress was laid on fresh air and exercise. It was these, she came to feel, that were the really important therapies; it was these she undertook to preach. But she did not cease her investigation of other remedies and of all the current developments of medical science. She read; she asked questions of all the informed people she met, and they were many, from Dr. Elizabeth Blackwell on; she made, whenever possible, firsthand investigation. She experimented with spirit rapping and animal magnetism, watched demonstrations of hypnosis, saw a table "with me on it" glide about the room, and devised ingenious tests for the authenticity of a clairvoyant. She concluded, and of course printed her conclusions, that the phenomena of spiritualism and magnetism were natural, not supernatural, that they should not, therefore, be accepted as bringing us knowledge of the future life, and that as therapy they should be used only with extreme caution.

In her pursuit of knowledge Catharine was likely to be quite ruthless with her friends. It never seemed to occur to her that they might be less concerned than she for the discovery and propagation of truth. The stimulating pleasure of Miss Beecher's acquaintance had too often to be paid for by the wearisome filling out of complicated reports or the laborious pacification of an irate cook whose favorite skillet had been ruined in the testing of a receipt. Yet if her friends suffered, the American public benefited by Catharine Beecher's wholehearted devotion to her cause, for her energetic mind worked over every phase of woman's life and set down instructive comment. *The American Woman's Home* proceeds from directions for building and equipping the house to advice on the good life to be lived there.

Again there is an excellent balance between general theory and particular detail. Miss Beecher covers such topics as Health of Mind, Giving in Charity, The Preservation of Good Temper in the Housekeeper, Social Duties, and Domestic Amusements.

The ceaseless parental problem of suitable entertainment for the young was especially acute in mid-nineteenth-century America when the weakening of

Calvinism was lifting restraints from conduct as well as modifying theology. Miss Beecher frankly admits that many of the positions she takes on amusements are debatable.

Dancing, she thinks, could be a healthful exercise though not as it is usually practiced in tight dresses in close rooms.

The acting of plays may be harmless and might be useful, but the position to be adopted here is that taken towards horse racing and circus riding which the Christian community is generally agreed to exclude. "Not because there is anything positively wrong in having men and horses run and perform feats of agility, or in persons looking on for diversion: but because experience has shown so many evils connected with these recreations, that they should be relinquished."

Card playing is one of the rare subjects on which Miss Beecher does not express a definite opinion. She merely remarks that "the sneer at biogotry and narrowness of views, on one side, and the uncharitable implication of want of piety, or sense, on the other, are equally ill-bred and unchristian."

On novel reading her opinion is definitely liberal and here again one feels the influence of Alexander Fisher who had bequeathed her his complete set of the Waverly novels. Fiction, she asserts, is certainly a permissible form of art since Jesus employs it in the parables but one must be on guard against novels which "throw the allurements of taste and genius around vice and crime." There are other snares also. The works of Dickens seem dangerous to her teacher's eye because of his false view of human nature, "as if such pure, elevated, refined characters could grow up under the most baleful influences, without parental influence, without education, and without religion: as if it made little or no difference with the human mind whether it were trained right or wrong, or not trained at all." How much novel reading young people should be permitted to do depends, Miss Beecher advises parents, on the individual temperament. To a dull and phlegmatic boy or girl, deficient in imagination, novels may be a useful stimulus, but a free indulgence in the excitements of fiction will, in the majority of cases, destroy the relish for more solid reading. These were the principles certainly on which Miss Beecher had regulated the debatable practice in her Hartford Seminary. She had committed herself to them still further in a preface to Harriet Beecher Stowe's *Mayflower Papers* which, in 1843, she collected and edited, launching the younger sister on her literary career.

The housekeeper's special virtues, economy, patience, neatness, which in the hands of most writers look dull and undesirable, take on life under Catharine Beecher's pen. She relates her admonitions to concrete situations and salts them with admirable common sense. In talking of economy, of both time and money, she suggests budgeting in the best modern manner, with helpful general rules for the week's tasks by which each housekeeper may lay out her own work scheme. Pertinent warnings are added, not only to the self-indulgent but also to the overconscientious, who are admonished that exercise, amusement, and "social enjoyment" are frequently "duty." Here is a characteristic paragraph on "The Preservation of Good Temper in the Housekeeper":

A very important consideration, is, that system, economy, and neatness are valuable, only so far as they tend to promote the comfort and well-being of those affected. Some women seem to act under the impression that these advantages *must* be secured, at all events, even if the comfort of the family be the sacrifice. True, it is very important that children grow up in habits of system, neatness, and order; and it is very desirable that the mother give them every incentive, both by precept and example; but it is still more important that they grow up with amiable tempers, that they learn to meet the crosses of life with patience and cheerfulness; and nothing has a greater influence to secure this than a mother's example. Whenever, therefore, a woman can not accomplish her plans of neatness and order without injury to her own temper or to the temper of others, she ought to modify and reduce them until she can.

Much of Catharine Beecher's power of propaganda lay in this realistic approach to domestic problems. The women who read her exhortations realized that she spoke from direct experience. They were influenced, too, because she was in her ideals so completely of her time. She moved in the front rank of her generation but not so far ahead of it as many of the reformers. Like most of her compatriots, she believed ardently that the world was on an upward path with America appointed to lead the nations towards a higher and happier life. Since this is true politically, she argued, we should feel called upon to advance also the health and well-being of mankind. It is surely inconsistent for the American people "to become slaves to injurious customs that are manufactured for them abroad." Why should they not originate customs in social life "as much in advance of old nations as are their civil concerns?" And when she needs to make a case for a particularly difficult virtue Miss Beecher adopts the tried American device of presenting it as synonymous with democracy. Early Rising, to which she devotes a whole chapter, becomes the symbol of a society in which all men share the work of the world. The late dinners and evening parties fashionable in England are signs of aristocratic decadence.

In almost every page of her book Catharine Beecher is thus breathing new life into the weary housekeeper by showing her that she is working in a great cause. Heartening, too, is the enthusiasm with which Miss Beecher approaches every detail of the daily round. It is an enthusiasm completely genuine. Much of woman's work seemed to her hard but none of it dull. (Very few things in life seemed to her dull.) She was thoroughly interested in the correct sloping of a seam in a "waist" and in discovering the best ways to cheer an aged invalid, in the proper making of a bed and the efficient care of a cow.

This unfeigned enthusiasm had much to do with her success as a teacher and as a propagandist. Unlike the abolitionists, the temperance workers, and women's rights leaders, who were working not only for freedom but against slavery, Catharine Beecher was entirely positive in her propaganda. She did not have to destroy, but only to arouse, and she never tired of arousing. All through this book, as through everything she wrote, she is expounding her doctrine both by implication and explicitly. She strikes off phrase after phrase designed to make the housekeeper feel the importance of her occupation:

"No statesman, at the head of a nation's affairs, has

more frequent calls for wisdom, firmness, tact, discrimination, prudence, and versatility of talent."

"A woman who has charge of a large household should regard her duties as dignified, important, and difficult."

"The prime minister of the family state."

And finally, in triumphant summary of woman's profession: "She who is the mother and housekeeper in a large family is the sovereign of an empire, demanding more varied cares, and involving more difficult duties, than are really exacted of her who wears a crown and professedly regulates the interests of the greatest nation on earth."

The house in Litchfield, drawn by Catharine Beecher

Beware of Sister Jane

JANE G. SWISSHELM

I DO really believe, Mr. Greeley, that it is a sin to be good-tempered." Jane Grey Swisshelm [Swíz-em] was only half in jest when she wrote that sentence in a dispatch to the New York *Tribune* describing the opening of the Senate press gallery to women. She had accomplished the reform, she said—the historic date is April 17, 1850—in "a fit of ill-temper." Most of the good work Mrs. Swisshelm did for her generation was done in anger and impatience, a righteous anger at injustice or cruelty or deceit, an impatience which made it impossible for her to sit quietly by when there was a battle to be fought.

Her desire to help in the bringing in of that better world in which nineteenth-century America so firmly believed made it necessary for Mrs. Swisshelm again and again to break through the stony barriers surrounding "woman's sphere." She was one of the first female editors in the country, one of the first women to act as a Washington correspondent. She was so unladylike as to lecture on a public platform. She had a desk in a publisher's office in a day when a nice woman put herself in a highly questionable position if she acted as secretary even for her own father. She was a Civil War nurse. She was a clerk in the Quartermaster's Office when the United States

Jane G. Swisshelm, a self-portrait, painted
probably in 1837

Government made its first experiments with women employees.

The deepest source of Jane Swisshelm's anger and the central focus of her energies was the great nineteenth-century cause, the battle for the freedom of the slave. She dedicated her efforts to abolition after she had spent a year in Kentucky, whose ground she saw as dark and bloody still. Her stories of her experience in Louisville are passionate firsthand reporting, far more horrifying to the modern reader than most of the carefully staged scenes in *Uncle Tom's Cabin*. Jane Swisshelm had always been an abolitionist in theory but this firsthand experience convinced her that God intended her to go down into the battle. The particular incident that crystalized this belief she relates in her autobiography:

She [my landlady] had an old, rheumatic cook, Martha, who seldom left her basement kitchen, except when she went to her Baptist meeting, but for hours and hours she crooned heart-breaking melodies of that hope within her, of a better and a happier world.

She had a severe attack of acute inflammation of the eyelids, which forcibly closed her eyes, and kept them closed; then she refused to work.

Her wages, one hundred and seventy-five dollars a year, were paid to her owner, a woman, and these went on; so her employer sent for her owner, and I, as an abolitionist, was summoned to the conference, that I might learn to pity the sorrows of mistresses, and understand the deceitfulness of slaves.

The injured owner sat in the shaded parlor, in a blue-black satin dress, that might almost have stood upright without assistance from the flesh or bones inside; with the dress was combined a mass of lace and jewelry that represented a large amount of money, and the mass as it sat there, and as I recall it, has made costly attire odious.

This bedizzoned martyr, this costumer's advertisement, sat and fanned as she recounted her grievances. Her entire allowance for personal expenses, was the wages of nine women, and her husband would not give her another dollar. They, knowing her necessities, were so ungrateful!—nobody could think how ungrateful; but in all her sorrows, Martha was her crowning grief. She had had two husbands, and had behaved so badly when the first was sold. Then, every time one of her thirteen children were disposed of, she "did take on so"; nobody could imagine "how she took on!"

Once, the gentle mistress had been compelled to send her to the workhouse and have her whipped by the constable; and that cost fifty cents; but really, this martyr and her husband had grown weary of flogging Martha. One hated so to send a servant to the public whipping-post; it looked like cruelty—did cruelly lacerate the feelings of refined people, and it was so ungrateful of Martha, and all the rest of them, to torture this fine lady in this rough way.

As to Martha's ingratitude, there could be no doubt; for to this our hostess testified, and called me to witness, that she had sent her a cup of tea every day since she had complained of being sick; yes, "a cup of tea with sugar in it," and yet the old wretch had not gone to work.

When they had finished the recital of their grievances they came down to business. The owner would remit two weeks' wages; after that it was the business of the employer to pay them, and see that they were earned. If it were necessary now to send Martha to the whipping-post, the lady in satin would pay the fifty cents; but for any future flogging, the lady in lawn must be responsible to the City of Louisville.

We adjourned to the kitchen where old Martha stood before her judge, clutching the table with her hard hands, trembling in every limb, her eyelids swollen out like puffballs, and offensive from neglect, her white curls making a border to her red turban, receiving her sentence without a word. As a sheep before her shearer she was dumb, opening not her mouth. Those wrinkled, old lips, from which I had heard few sounds, save those of prayer and praise, were closed by a cruelty perfectly incomprehensible in its unconscious debasement. Our hostess was a leading member of the Fourth St. M.E. Church, the other feminine fiend a Presbyterian.

I promised the Lord then and there, that for life, it should be my work to bring "deliverance to the captive, and the opening of the prison to them that are bound," but all I could do for Martha, was to give her such medical treatment as would restore her sight and save her from the whipping-post, and this I did.

That account was written nearly twenty years after the signing of the Emancipation Proclamation but Jane Swisshelm's anger towards the feminine fiends had not yet cooled. Her anger seldom did. That was part of her special power of persuasion. Most of the women who labored for abolition or temperance or woman's rights were skillful at keeping their tempers. They had plenty of courage; they suffered and endured; but they remained soft spoken, meek, and femininely persuasive; they reasoned with their enemies. Mrs. Swisshelm knocked hers down. She struck shrewdly, courageously, and without respect of persons. Her reporting filled a function accepted as important by the modern press, a function always important to a democracy: she cried upon the housetops deeds which public figures supposed they had shut safely away in closets. When the public figures turned upon their accuser with abuse she replied in kind, and better than kind, for she was an adept at mockery and scorn. This useful venom of hers was distilled in Jane Swisshelm by the thwarting of two fine passions: her strong natural affection and her desire to paint portraits. Her parents and her brother died when she was young; her sister married and went West; her only child was born late in her married life; and her marriage was the result of a bizarre romantic attraction to a character wholly incompatible with hers. Portrait painting, which was her true vocation, she foreswore because when she had a brush in her hand she forgot to cook the dinner.

Had she been a conventional nineteenth-century lady we should never have learned of these vital griefs. The well-bred female of her day did not set down personal and family matters in print. When, for instance, that excellent Victorian Mrs. Oliphant followed her stream of novels with an autobiography, she remarked, after speaking of the feckless brother whose son she put through Eton by the labor of her indefatigable pen, that none of us can "ever really tell what were perhaps the best and most creditable things in our own life, since by the strange fate which attends us human creatures, what is most creditable to one is often least creditable to another. . . . all can never be told of any family story, except at the cost of family honour."

That was the correct point of view but when Mrs. Swisshelm, at sixty-five, began to write her autobiography, after she had retired from journalism and combat, after the slaves had been freed, the Union wounded healed, and the bloodthirsty Indians of Minnesota subdued, she spoke in a different vein. Sitting alone in her old stone house in Swissvale, Pennsylvania, with competence enough for her frugal living, she called up her past and put it down on paper not at all in the manner of Mrs.

Oliphant, rather in the manner of the generation of Virginia Woolf.

The book opens with two brief paragraphs on Jane's first memories: a visual memory of sitting, at the age of two, under a shower of apple blossoms; and a moral memory, the seering experience, at three, of the sense of sin. The narrative has no Victorian discursiveness or *longueurs*. Some of the important scenes towards the end of the Half Century are described in vivid reportorial detail but the emotions and events of girlhood and marriage emerge obliquely, by implication, in strange half-lights.

Jane Grey Cannon was born December 6, 1815, in Pittsburgh, which was then a little city of less than five thousand. Her parents were Scotch-Irish Calvinists and that serious fighting faith which darkened and strengthened her childhood set in her for life the obligation to right a wrong when she saw it. Her father died when she was seven but an ingenious and indomitable mother kept a shop, made leghorn bonnets, and cured two children of incipient tuberculosis by moving her family to the country (Wilkinsburg) where she nourished them on fresh air, light gardening, and the "gentle use of dumb-bells."

Jane was a tiny creature, clever with her hands, clever with her head, and, apparently, pretty. At the age of eight she was swelling the family income by giving instruction in the current fad of lace making, conducting her lessons seated on the laps of her young lady pupils. At fourteen she was teaching school.

She gives a Jane Eyre description of her first meeting with the black-browed young giant who insisted on marrying her when she was twenty-one. His romantic appearance and qualities seem to have entirely blinded her usual shrewd discernment. She was quite unaware of his weaknesses and his stupidities though she saw clearly enough that, because of religious differences, their union might not be altogether harmonious. James Swisshelm's mother was an ardent camp-meeting Methodist while Jane's ideal of wifely subservience, high as it was, stopped short of the relinquishment of her Presbyterian tenets.

Her lover pointed out that he was not himself a church member and promised that she might always attend her own meeting. He said also that she need not live in his mother's household; he would take her up the river into the woods and start a sawmill. Lumbering was his business. But these plans were circumvented by his shrewd Methodist mother. She converted James just before the wedding, November 18, 1836; then together mother and son began to labor to save the soul of the bride and make her, since she was so clever, into a Methodist preacher. The first step was to bring her into residence in the Swisshelm matriarchal household. Jane resisted. She continued to live with her own mother; then she lived at her husband's mill and kept house for his hired man. There were quarrels and scenes and recriminations; her husband threatened suicide. At last he broke away from his mother and took Jane South, to Louisville, where his brother had established a lumber business. When the business failed Jane supported her husband by making corsets, until word came that her own mother was dying of cancer. Swisshelm forbade her to go home but Jane felt that in this instance her husband's command was clean contrary to the law of God. She boarded a steamer for the North.

All through her married life Jane Swisshelm was torn by these conflicts between her ingrained belief that a wife owes submissive obedience to her husband and her clear perception that what her husband required of her was too often at variance with the right. Her reverence for the divine law was rooted not only in parental teaching but in thoughtful personal conviction. Only in middle life did travel and wider horizons and the changing thought of her generation show her that she could retain her religion even if she ceased to believe in the verbal inspiration of the Bible. During her young womanhood she felt it essential to render literal obedience to all the Pauline anti-feminist dicta. She longed to cry aloud the horrors of slavery but she was convinced that no woman ought to speak from a public platform. She truly believed that "the husband is the head of the wife," and when she found her mind developing more rapidly than Swisshelm's she adopted a course which to the twentieth-century matron appears almost too fantastic to believe:

I knew from the first that his education had been limited, but thought the defect would be easily remedied as he had good abilities, but I discovered he had no love for books. His spiritual guides derided human learning and depended on inspiration. My knowledge stood in the way of my salvation, and I must be that odious thing—a superior wife—or stop my progress, for to be and appear were the same thing. I must be the mate of the man I had chosen; and if he would not come to my level, I must go to his. So I gave up study, and for years did not read one page in any book save the Bible.

Yet another and sharper sacrifice she made to the nineteenth-century code of womanhood. She denied her true vocation as an artist, a painter of portraits. As a very little girl she had excelled in the elegant art of painting on velvet and she was always skillful with a needle or at any work with her hands, but she had never seen a picture or met a painter until, shortly after her marriage, a traveling artist came to Wilkinsburg. "We visited his studio, and a new world opened to me. . . . when I saw a portrait on the easel, a palette of paints and some brushes, I was at home in a new world, at the head of a long vista of faces which I must paint; but the aspiration was another secret to keep."

Bard, her husband's hired man, made her a stretcher and, with a yard of unbleached muslin, some tacks, and white lead, she constructed a canvas. Oil, turpentine, and paints in primary colors were in the shop where she was keeping house for Bard. She set to work on a portrait of her husband, hiding it when he was there or when she heard anyone coming. Once she blistered it badly trying to dry it before the fire. She realized that it was "a very rough work," but

it was a portrait, a daub, a likeness, and the hand was his hand and no other. The figure was correct, and the position in the chair, and from the moment when I began it, I felt I had found my vocation.

What did I care for preachers and theological arguments? What matter who sent me my bread, or whether I had any? What matter for anything, so long as I had a canvas and some paints, with that long perspective of faces and figures crowding up and begging to be painted. The face of every one I knew was there, with every line and varying expression, and in each I seemed to read the inner life in the outer form. Oh, how they plead with me! What graceful lines and gorgeous colors floated around me! I forgot God, and did not know it; forgot philosophy, and did not care to remember it; but alas! I forgot to get Bard's dinner, and, although I forgot to be hungry, I had no reason to suppose he did. He would willingly have gone hungry, rather than give any one trouble; but I had neglected a duty. Not only once did I do this, but again and again, the fire went out or the bread ran over in the pans, while I painted and dreamed.

My conscience began to trouble me. Housekeeping was "woman's sphere," although I had never then heard the words, for no woman had gotten out of it, to be hounded back; but I knew my place, and scorned to leave it. I tried to think I could paint without neglect of duty. It did not occur to me that painting was a duty for a married woman! Had the passion seized me before marriage, no other love could have come between me and art; but I felt that it was too late, as my life was already devoted to another object—housekeeping.

It was a hard struggle. I tried to compromise, but experience soon deprived me of that hope, for to paint was to be oblivious of all other things. In my doubt, I met one of those newspaper paragraphs with which men are wont to pelt women into subjection: "A man does not marry an artist, but a housekeeper." This fitted my case, and my doom was sealed.

I put away my brushes; resolutely crucified my divine gift, and while it hung writhing on the cross, spent my best years and powers cooking cabbage.

Just one picture painted by Jane Swisshelm remains to us, a self-portrait, now in the possession of the Historical Society of Western Pennsylvania.

Though she might shut off its natural outlet, Jane Swisshelm's need for expression continued strong and, since her husband could share so few of her thoughts, it became all the more necessary to pour them out on paper. She began to write stories and rhymes and found a ready market for them in Philadelphia papers, the *Dollar Magazine* and *Neal's Saturday Gazette*. She signed them, as propriety demanded of a lady, with a pseudonym, "Jennie

[sic] Deans." She wrote also for the *Spirit of Liberty*, an anti-slavery weekly published in Pittsburgh, sending the editor articles on abolition and on "woman's right to life, liberty, and the pursuit of happiness."

Writing never so engrossed Jane Swisshelm that she forgot to cook the dinner but it did relieve her soul a little. Only a little, however; the perpetual irritation and misunderstanding engendered by Methodism and her mother-in-law brought on at last a quarrel with her husband so terrible that she attempted to leave his house forever. She was prevented by well-meaning friends who "brought down the lever of scripture and conscience," but the cumulated emotional strain produced a serious nervous collapse.

For weeks she lay on a sickbed going over and over in her mind the details of her wretched state, beating her brains to find its origin. Suddenly it flashed upon her: her sufferings were a judgment of God because she had done so little for the cause to which she had vowed herself in Kentucky, the cause of the slave. The citizen of nineteenth-century America could seldom pass comfortably by on the other side. Evil was not insuperable, too great for human strength. It could be overcome and it was one's duty therefore to attack it.

Jane Swisshelm could not lift her head from the pillow but she began at once her abolitionist campaign. She called for a pencil and scrawled a half column of verse in which she attacked by name certain Methodist preachers, frequent visitors to her house, who had been responsible for the passing by their church of the "Black Gag" rule. This curious statute forbade colored members of the congregation to testify in church courts against white members, thus making it impossible for a slave seeking protection from the cruelty of a master to present his case to the judgment of the church.

Mrs. Swisshelm sent off her verse to the Pittsburgh *Spirit*, signing it with her initials but telling the editor that he might give her full name if it were asked for. This was to her mind a really shocking procedure. Her mother had trained her to belief in the contemporary dictum that a lady's name is seen in the papers only twice: when she marries and when she dies. "I can understand," Jane Swisshelm wrote years later (in the course of a letter to the New York *Tribune*, May 28, 1850), "because I have experienced the feeling, why a young girl should hesitate to be married, from extreme dread of seeing her name in a newspaper."

The Pittsburgh *Spirit* printed the verses with "Jane G. Swisshelm" in full beneath them, and a great outcry arose. The preachers whom she had pilloried threatened suit but two anti-slavery lawyers in Pittsburgh rallied to her defense and the matter was eventually dropped.

Having found this blow for the cause effective Mrs. Swisshelm was tempted to go upon the lecture platform and speak for abolition but again her Presbyterian training intervened. St. Paul, more than anyone except Queen Victoria, was responsible for the pattern of female behavior in the nineteenth century. There is scarcely a strong-minded woman who has not set down in some letter or diary the soul searching she found necessary when she determined to defy the command that women should keep silence in the churches. Even Margaret Fuller wrote, in 1832, that the gift she would choose would be eloquence, "if I were a man." One of the purposes of her autobiography, Mrs. Swisshelm stated in the preface, was "to illustrate the force of education and the mutability of human character, by a personal narrative of one who, . . . in 1837, could not break the seal of silence set upon her lips by 'Inspiration,' even so far as to pray with a man dying of intemperance, and who yet, in 1862, addressed the Minnesota Senate in session."

In 1845 the force of education was just beginning to work and Jane Swisshelm felt that she might plead for the slave only with her pen. She did feel obliged to sign every article she sent to the Pittsburgh *Commercial Journal*, for nearly everything she wrote was libelous since she employed the feminine, and effective, practice of reducing political and social principles to personal terms. Her careful honesty, oddly enough, proved a protection. Her name as written looked so improbable that it was generally accepted as a pseudonym. There was even a rumor that it cloaked a certain liberal member of the state legislature.

While fighting for the slave Jane Swisshelm struck blows also for the rights of woman. After an argument with her husband over the disposition of her mother's estate it occurred to her that "all the advances made by humanity had been through the pressure of injustice, and that the screws had been turned on me that I might do something to right the great wrong which forbade a married woman to own property." She sent to the *Journal* a series of letters which were materially responsible for the passage by the Pennsylvania Legislature of a married woman's property act, one of the earliest in the country. Not long after the measure went through, a young Ohio lawyer asked for an introduction that he might congratulate her on her achievement. She marked him, not unnaturally, as a young man who would go far—and later encountered Edwin Stanton in Washington as Secretary of War to President Lincoln.

In the fall of 1847 an abolitionist paper, the *Albatross*, was started in Pittsburgh and Jane Swisshelm was asked to write for it. She declined because the publisher of the *Journal* objected, "and the *Journal* had five hundred readers for every one the *Albatross* could hope. [The population of Pittsburgh was then about 21,000.] In the one I reached the ninety and nine unconverted, while in the other I must talk principally to those who were rooted and grounded in the faith." So she continued to write letters for the *Journal* until one day she heard casually from a friend that the *Albatross* was printing its last issue. The publisher's funds were exhausted and the citizens of Pittsburgh seemed too hostile to the cause to support an abolition paper. Impulsively Mrs. Swisshelm cried that she would start a paper herself. She had that little legacy from her mother's estate. "I wish you would," said her friend enthusiastically. "You can make a go of it if anybody can."

Swiftly she made her plans. Her husband agreed. He was a sincere abolitionist—one of the few points at which they were in accord; he admired his wife's ability; and he thought she might as well have for herself the money the *Journal* was making out of her letters. Jane Swisshelm went to Robert Riddle, publisher of the *Journal*, and told him she was going to start the Pittsburgh *Saturday Visiter* as an organ for the Liberty party. The first copy, she said, must be issued Saturday week so that the abolitionists should not have time to become discouraged, and she wanted him to print her paper.

He was horrified at the idea. "Are you insane?" he asked. He assured her that the project was ruinous, begged her to take time to think; finally he raised a point which she had not considered. "You would have to furnish a desk for yourself, you see there is but one in this room, and there is no other place for you. You could not conduct a paper and stay at home, but must spend a good deal of time here!"

I suddenly saw the appalling prospect thus politely presented. I had never heard of any woman save Mary Kingston working in an office. Her father, a prominent lawyer, had employed her as his clerk, when his office was in their dwelling, and the situation was remarkable and very painful; and here was I, looking not more than twenty, proposing to come into the office of the handsome stranger who sat bending over his desk that he might not see me blush for the unwomanly intent.

Jane Swisshelm blushed but she did not shrink. "This," she thought, "is my Red Sea. It can be no more terrible than the one which confronted Israel. Duty lies on the other side, and I am going over! 'Speak unto the children of Israel that they go forward!' The crimson waves of scandal, the white foam of gossip, shall part before me and heap themselves up as walls on either hand."

"Speak unto the children of Israel that they go forward!" She set that line at the *Visiter's* masthead. (She overrode Mr. Riddle also on the spelling of *Visiter*, her version being Dr. Johnson's.)

The first copy of the Pittsburgh *Saturday Visiter* was

presented to the public on January 20, 1848. It was a six-column weekly with a small Roman letterhead, "quite an insignificant looking sheet, but no sooner did the American eagle catch sight of it, than he swooned and fell off his perch. Democratic roosters straightened out their necks and ran screaming with terror. Whig coons scampered up trees and barked furiously. . . . A woman had started a political paper! A woman!"

The scandal of a woman's escaping from her sphere loomed larger at first than the presence of a new organ of abolition. George D. Prentiss of the Louisville *Courier* summed up the general distress when he cried, in the course of a two-third column leader: "She is a man all but the pantaloons." Mrs. Swisshelm replied with a brief rhyme so cutting that it caused a fellow editor to give a warning often thereafter quoted, "Brother George, beware of sister Jane."

It was during the years of her editorship of the *Visiter* that Mrs. Swisshelm established her reputation as a journalist. The paper began with three subscribers and during the first year cost its publisher several hundred dollars but by 1851 the subscription list was well over six thousand and the *Visiter* was circulating in every state in the Union. Not all its readers were paying customers, or even willing ones. Mrs. Swisshelm took good care to send the *Visiter* to a list of Southern editors who continually denounced its "prejudice" and "injustice" but were obliged as they did so to copy in their columns many paragraphs of her "abolition rant." She had a long free list also of distinguished men in public life and week after week her articles were copied by admiring contemporaries, for the nineteenth-century editor, having no boilerplate to pad his pages, availed himself freely of the work of fellow journalists.

Lady editors took particular pleasure in reprinting from the *Visiter*. Those more temperate and pacific strong-minded women, laboring to inherit the earth by meekness, found a vicarious strength in Mrs. Swisshelm. She "does use up such chaps as that Mirror man *so* nicely!" chuckles Mrs. Bloomer reprinting in her *Lily* a letter in defense of the Worcester suffrage convention.

It was not often that Mrs. Swisshelm could be quoted in defense of the suffrage cause for she did not believe in the immediate necessity of the ballot. She thought it an "all powerful weapon," but she said that the suffragists were trying to get too much at once. She was highly critical, too, of their conventions and other methods of propaganda which she found inept and amateurish. Mathilda Gage's *History of Woman's Suffrage* speaks bitterly of the tone in which *Half a Century* discusses the Suffrage Association but it was merely the tone in which Mrs. Swisshelm discussed most organized reform. She believed in temperance, but thought signing pledges a "lying-made-easy invention"; she deplored the stupidities of women's dress, but did not like the bloomer costume. She was usually too impatient and intolerant to work effectively within a group; she thought faster than most people and did not suffer fools gladly.

The period of the *Visiter* [she wrote] was one of great mental activity—a period of hobbies—and it, having assumed the reform roll, was expected to assume all the reforms. Turkish trowsers, Fourierism, Spiritualism, Vegetarianism, Phonetics, Pneumonics, the Eight Hour Law, Criminal Caudling [coddling], Magdalenism, and other devices for teaching pyramids to stand on their apex were pressed upon the *Visiter*, and it was held by the disciples of each as "false to all its professions," when declining to devote itself to its advocacy. There were a thousand men and women, who knew exactly what it ought to do; but seldom two of them agreed, and none ever thought of furnishing funds for the doing of it. Reformers insisted that it should advocate their plan of hurrying up the millennium, furnish the white paper and pay the printers. Fond parents came with their young geniuses to have them baptized in type from the *Visiter* font. Male editors were far away folks, but the *Visiter* would sympathize with family hopes.

Yet this very sharpness of Jane Swisshelm's delighted the reformers whenever she was ready to engage in battle on their side. Her opponents seem to have been really afraid of her pen. Particularly disconcerting to the masculine mind was her practice of making personal application of general ideas. When, for instance, her good friend Robert Riddle counseled in his *Journal* obedience to the Fugitive Slave Law inasmuch as it was a law of the land, Mrs. Swisshelm imagined a scene in which a scantily clad woman, with bruised and bleeding feet, clasping an infant to her bosom, ran up Third Street in Pittsburgh, panting before her pursuers.

The master called on all good citizens for help. The cry reached the ears of the tall editor of the *Journal* seated at his desk. He dropped his pen, hastily donned his new brass collar and started in hot pursuit of this wicked woman, who was feloniously appropriating the property of her master.

The other Riddle [the similarity of name was a mere coincidence]—the Presbyterian pastor—planted himself by the lamp post on the corner of Third and Market streets, and with spectacles on nose and raised hands, loudly implored divine blessing on the labors of his tall namesake.

The *Visiter* concluded by advising masters who had slaves to catch, to apply to these gentlemen, who would attend to the business from purely pious and patriotic motives. A few weeks later Robert Riddle came to Mrs. Swisshelm in distress, demanding that she make some retraction; he had already had three letters from the South asking him to help in returning fugitive slaves to their masters. The *Visiter* duly announced that it had been mistaken in saying that either of the Riddles would aid in returning fugitives. "They both scorned the business, and Robt. M., would cut off his right hand, rather than engage in it. He only meant that other people should do what would degrade him."

People who knew Jane Swisshelm only from paragraphs of this sort always imagined her a tall and violent Amazon; "a cross between a woman and a tigress," one clerical college president called her. But people who met her face to face use in describing her words like "winning," "quiet," "retiring"; not adjectives certainly which anyone would apply to her prose. We know that she was tiny, only five feet tall and never weighing more than a hundred pounds; that her eyes were a liquid blue, her brown hair parted in the middle and waved softly over a "noble" forehead; her mouth small and her teeth fine, her smile "truly enchanting." "Quite a Jenny Lind in appearance," said one reporter. Her speaking voice was low and pleasant.

This gentle Amazon, like most of the other strong-minded women, enjoyed writing on domestic topics. Cartoonists to the contrary, the emancipated female seldom neglected her household duties. As a matter of fact, she performed them rather better than most of her homekeeping sisters for she took them with professional seriousness. Uncowed by tradition she examined current ideas of diet, dress, and interior decoration, discovered better methods of procedure, and then felt compelled, since she believed human nature perfectable, to urge them on her fellow housewives. Most popular of Mrs. Swisshelm's domestic pronunciamentoes was a series of "Letters to Country Girls" which she ran in the *Visiter* in 1849 and 1850. They were published as a book in 1854.

In these Letters Mrs. Swisshelm drops the editorial "we." She speaks like an older sister giving, with affectionate impatience, advice garnered from her own experience. She discusses reading, health, diet, dress, and how to make yourself pretty, mingling general advice with specific instruction, in the knitting of gloves, for instance, to wear while you hoe and so preserve your hands, or the proper shaping of the gusset seam in a "waist."

Not one mantuamaker in fifty knows how to make it, for not one in fifty knows how to draw a portrait. I would let no woman cut and make a dress for me who had not the natural talents for a portrait painter. A dress-maker should be an artist—one who knows and can draw all the graceful curves in the outline of a human form, such an one will never make a seam in the waist of a dress that can be marked with a straight rule.

An indication, this, that Jane Swisshelm had not ceased to think in terms of the art she had forbidden herself to practice.

Clear proof that the name Jane G. Swisshelm was

nationally known is the important position Horace
Greeley gave her work whenever he published it in the
Tribune. In 1850, when Mrs. Swisshelm told him that she
wanted to go to Washington, he immediately offered her
$5 a column and ran her correspondence in conspicuous
positions under large heads: "Letter from Mrs. Swisshelm." The Letters are by no means conventional reporting. They are individual and opinionated in the style of
the modern columnist. The writing is easy and lively,
amusing sometimes, sometimes angry, always full of gusto.
It was because she made life seem exciting that people
liked to read Jane Swisshelm.

Her first Washington Letter (published April 12, 1850)
describes the "sublimity" of the national capital and the
curious contrast of its grandeur with the wretched
countryside of Maryland. This wretchedness Mrs. Swisshelm sees of course as the result of slaveholding and slave
labor. Her descriptions of scenery have, almost invariably,
social implications. She indulges in none of the nature
rhapsodies of her contemporaries. She wanted to be a
portrait, not a landscape painter. Even when she admires
a prospect, as she often did, especially in Minnesota, her
figures and her adjectives are perfunctory until her imagination begins to run a railroad through the plain or along
the high plateau. It is not pictures which interest her but
ideas, and most of her ideas are concerned with reform.
She felt strongly her generation's compulsion to right the
wrongs of the world, and to right them quickly. The
anger in which she wrote so much of the time had an excellent influence on her style. It saved her from feminine
gush and coyness; it drove her straight and surely to her
points, freeing her from the prolixities and trivialities of

her contemporaries; it made her humor so satirical that it is seldom silly and only occasionally dates.

The second Washington Letter (published April 15) is concerned with a Senate debate on the Fugitive Slave Law but it is not so much a report on what was said as an answer to it and a commentary. "They keep such a dingdong about 'supporting the Constitution.' One might imagine it was some miserable, decrepit old creature that was no longer able to totter on crutches but must be held up on every side, and dragged along like a drunken loafer, on his road to the lock-up."

The third Letter (April 19) gives an excited description of the incident in the Senate Chamber when Foote drew a pistol against Thomas Hart Benton.

The Letter of April 22 recounts Mrs. Swisshelm's historic invasion of the Senate press gallery, a fine blow for female freedom which she presents as the result of a fit of temper:

You know what a miserable, contemptible, paltry excuse for a gallery there is in the U.S. Senate—a thing like a berth on a canal-boat, hung up near the top, about six feet wide, and partitioned into two rows of seats, with no way of getting into them but by walking over people who are already there, and who are always sure to be too rude either to move forward to a vacant seat or stand up to allow others to pass. I never was in it but twice, and once I witnessed a scene there, between the wifes of honorable members, that would be disgraceful to a Western huckster woman. I saw the wife of a Senator refuse to rise and permit the wife of a Member of the House to pass to a vacant seat on the ladies' row, and thus compel her to crowd through the solid mass of men that always blocks up the seat. I saw ladies walk over the seats and step over the back of them to get out or in, while men and women refused to move an inch. I would rather force my way through a crowded horsemarket and sit on the auctioneer's block, than go into the gallery again. . . . So I determined, like the poor lover when his lady-love threw him into the swill-barrel, "I'll never go there any more." But I could not thus resign all purpose of seeing the American Senate, and so sought an introduction to Mr. FILLMORE, made a formal application for a reporter's desk, and it was granted at once, "*The Republic*" reporters very kindly resigning one of their desks to my use. Yesterday I occupied it for the first time, and thus had a fine opportunity of seeing the FOOTE and BENTON affray. Mrs. SOUTHWORTH, the author of "Retribution," and my dear friend, went with me, and to-day I have two ladies of this city by the invitation of the gentlemanly reporter, Mr. Andrews, simply to sustain the precedent. So much for a fit of ill-temper! It has established woman's right to sit as a reporter in our legislative halls. I should not have thought of it, if they had not made me angry, and I do really believe, Mr. Greeley, that it is a sin to be good-tempered.

Despite her lively curiosity and her swift, close observation Jane Swisshelm was not an ideal reporter; she was inaccurate about details and she was frequently gullible, particularly where anything discreditable to the slave-owning South was concerned. She believed that President Taylor had been poisoned with a plate of strawberries because he would not sign the Fugitive Slave bill, and that President Harrison had likewise been secretly assassinated by Southern treachery. When Daniel Webster urged the passage of the Fugitive Slave Law as a means of preserving the Union she felt that his greatness was rotten at the core and she accepted as fact the tale of a "family of eight mulattoes, bearing the image and superscription of the great New England statesman, who paid the rent and grocery bills of their mother as regularly as he did those of his wife."

She decided finally that it was her duty to expose Webster's true character to his constituents and she published the story in her *Visiter*. She knew that after the tale had appeared in print Greeley would no longer care to have her as a correspondent so, as she tells it in her autobiography, she immediately left the capital. The letter she sent to the *Tribune* on May 24 explains that a serious illness made it necessary for her to return to her home.

For all its political success and national importance the *Visiter* could not make ends meet. A brother-in-law who undertook the business management, for which Mrs. Swisshelm felt that she had no time, finally ran the paper entirely into the ground and it was decided to combine it with Riddle's *Journal* (1852). Mrs. Swisshelm continued to write for the *Family Journal and Visiter* until the spring of 1857 when she reached a crisis in her domestic affairs. She decided to leave her husband. He would not consent to a legal separation and, though he did not dare to oppose her determination to take their six-year-old daughter with her, he did prevent her moving any of her personal property. What little she managed to carry away had to be taken out of the house by stealth.

On May 20 Jane Swisshelm and little Nettie (Mary Henrietta) embarked for Minnesota where Jane's only relative, her younger sister Elizabeth Mitchell, and her husband had settled in St. Cloud. Three years later James Swisshelm obtained a divorce from his wife on grounds of desertion. "In '70 he married again, and I having, voluntarily, assumed the legal guilt of breaking my marriage contract, do cheerfully accept the legal penalty—a life of celibacy—bringing no charge against him who was my husband, save that he was not much better than the average man."

Jane Swisshelm's plan for her life in Minnesota was mildly romantic but adequately practical. Her brother-in-law Henry Z. Mitchell had taken up in her name some forty acres of land on the shore of a lovely little lake about twelve miles from St. Cloud. There she intended to build a cabin "of tamarac logs, with the bark on and the ends sticking out at the corners criss-cross," plant a garden, catch fish, raise poultry, and enjoy two sensations of which her married life had given her no taste, peace and solitude. An occasional Fenimore Cooper Indian moved picturesquely across the canvas of her daydream and she made him her everlasting friend by giving him food or caring for his sick children. But, alas, just as she arrived in Minnesota the troops, stationed through the state to protect the settlers against the Sioux, were ordered to Kansas to put down the Free State party. For a woman to live alone in the forest would, she learned, be utterly foolhardy, and Jane Swisshelm was too intelligent to be foolhardy. Reluctantly she abandoned her tamarac cabin and settled down in St. Cloud with her brother and sister.

Not long after she took up residence in Minnesota Mrs. Swisshelm began to look about for some means of earning an income. She practiced the independence she preached and had no intention of being permanently beholden to even the kindest of brothers-in-law. Journalism of course suggested itself and the owner of a defunct newspaper proposed that Mrs. Swisshelm revive it for him, offering her payment in town lots. She told him that if she edited a paper it must express her own opinions and that the community might not like her abolitionism. George Brott laughed; if she could recommend Minnesota to immigrants and St. Cloud as a town site she might have what politics she pleased. So the St. Cloud *Visiter* was launched, carrying the name of Jane Swisshelm's first paper and its motto: "Speak unto the Children of Israel, that they go forward." The editor suspected that she might be on the shore of another Red Sea but it was not until some weeks later that she began to hear its thunder.

General—that is, Adjutant General—Sylvanus B. Lowry, Democratic boss of Minnesota, made his home in St. Cloud, where he lived "in a semi-barbaric splendor, in an imposing house on the bank of the Mississippi, where he kept slaves, bringing them from and returning them to his Tennessee estate, at his convenience, and no man saying him nay." When Mrs. Swisshelm solicited for her paper the support of local magnates General Lowry wrote that he would give her support such as no paper in the district had ever had if she would back Buchanan's administration. She answered meekly that the *Visiter* could not live without General Lowry's support so she would do as he requested. Horror, on the part of friends and relatives, when Lowry began to boast about the town that he had bought the new paper. Jane Swisshelm's friends seem always to have felt a vicarious need for her belligerency; they could not bear to have her knuckle under. There was Republican rejoicing, therefore, when it became clear that she had not capitulated after all but was again fighting tyranny with feminine wiles. She kept her promise to support Buchanan with a literalness which even Lowry's astute mind could not have anticipated.

On February 18, 1858, an editorial in the *Visiter* announced that the paper would in future support Buchanan's administration and went on to state the objects of that administration as being:

the entire subversion of Freedom and the planting of Slavery in every State and Territory, so that Toombs could realize his boast, and call the roll of his slaves at the foot of Bunker Hill. . . . Henry Clay had said that Northern workingmen were "mudsills, greasy mechanics and small-fisted farmers." These mudsills had been talking of voting themselves farms; but it would be much more appropiate if they would vote themselves masters. Southern laborers were blessed with kind masters, and Mr. Buchanan and the St. Cloud *Visiter* were most anxious that Northern laborers should be equally well provided for.

The second number of Buchanan's organ (March 4) explained how it was that Mrs. Swisshelm became a supporter of a policy she had long opposed:

Gen. Lowry owned Northern Minnesota, land and inhabitants, bought folks up as fast as they came to it, and had bought me. He was going to support the *Visiter* in great power and glory, if it gave satisfaction as a democratic organ. I would work hard for the money, and it would be odd if any one gave Mr. Buchanan a more enthusiastic support than I. Indeed, I was his only honest supporter. All the others pretended he was going to do something quite foreign to his purpose, while I was in his confidence. The one sole object of his administration was the perpetuation and spread of slavery, and this object the *Visiter* would support with the best arguments in its power.

Lowry was furious. He gave orders that Jane Swisshelm was to be suppressed and the man he appointed for the office was his personal attorney James C. Shepley. The form of attack Shepley chose could have been imagined only on the American frontier. He announced that on March 10 he would give a public lecture on "Woman."

The parlors of the Stearns House were crowded, those parlors where the gold framed mirrors, ormolu clocks, and lustered chandeliers, laboriously transported by train, stage, and steamboat, announced the local glory that was to be. The citizens of St. Cloud came dressed in their most elegant costumes.

The lecturer divided his subject into four parts: the coquette, the flirt, the old maid, and the strong-minded woman who dabbled in politics. He described each type in witty detail and in each he found some extenuating virtues—except in the strong-minded woman. No individual names were mentioned but the application was unmistakable. Several times Mrs. Swisshelm's brother-in-law leaped to his feet to retaliate but she pulled him down and the vociferous claque of General Lowry's followers made it appear that everything the lecturer said was thoroughly acceptable to his audience. The Democrats were so delighted with the effect that they gathered after the lecture for a lively party in celebration of their victory.

The next issue of the St. Cloud *Visiter* reviewed Mr. Shepley's discourse as calmly as though it had been a purely abstract discussion. The editor praised his understanding of the female sex but pointed out that his classification omitted one important type, the frontier belle,

the large, thick-skinned, coarse, sensual-featured, loud-mouthed double-fisted dame, whose entrance into a room appears to take one's breath, whose conversational tones are audible at the furthest side of the next square, whose guffahs resound across a mile wide river, and who talks with an energy which makes the saliva fly like—showers of melted pearls. . . . Her triumphs consist in card-table successes, displays of cheap finery, and in catching a marriageable husband for herself and her poor relations.

This description fitted Mrs. Shepley rather more accurately than Shepley's caricature of the strong-minded woman had described Mrs. Swisshelm and, with a certain inconsistency, he rose to the defense of womanhood. On March 24 three men—eventually identified as Lowry, Shepley, and Dr. Benjamin Palmer, engaged to Mrs. Shepley's sister—broke into the *Visiter* office, destroyed the press, scattered some of the type about the street and threw the rest into the Mississippi. On the office table they left a note:

The citizens of St. Cloud have determined to abate the nuisance of which you have made the "Visiter" a striking specimen.

They have decided that it is fit only for the inmates of Brothels, and you seem to have had some experience of the tastes of such persons.

You will never have the opportunity to repeat the offence in this town, without paying a more serious penalty than you do now.

By order of the Committee of Vigilance

The citizens of St. Cloud who were not members of Lowry's gang were outraged by this action. "Men walked down to the bank of the great Mississippi, looked at the little wrecked office standing amid the old primeval forest, as if it were a great battle-ground, and the poor little type were the bodies of the valiant dead." The men of St. Cloud were Democrats, most of them, and they did not believe in abolition but they did believe in American liberty, fair play, and a free press, and they cared for the good name of their town. They called a mass meeting to be held that evening, in the parlors of the Stearns House where Shepley had delivered his lecture on "Woman." Mrs. Swisshelm said that she would be present and herself give an account of the *Visiter's* contest with General Lowry. She would speak in public; she felt at last a compulsion stronger than the bonds of St. Paul.

She made her will, settled her business affairs, wrote a statement of the controversy, "that it might live if I ceased to do so." Then she sent for Miles Brown, "a Pennsylvanian, who had the reputation of being a dead shot, and had a pair of fine revolvers. He pledged himself solemnly to go with me and keep near me, and shoot me square through the brain, if there was no other way of preventing me falling alive into the hands of the mob."

The Stearns House was packed that evening, parlors, halls, and stairs. Outside milled a crowd with General Lowry at their head. Several prominent members of the community spoke; then Mrs. Swisshelm mounted the rostrum, which had been erected at the end of the parlor but moved when it was found that the speaker's head came in tempting range of a shot through the front door.

The crowds inside and out were quiet while Mrs. Swisshelm read her report, until she named Lowry, Shepley, and Palmer as the persons who had wrecked the *Visiter* office. Then there was a howl of oaths and catcalls. A rush was made, stones hurled against the house, and pistols fired. When the mob had been pressed back and comparative quiet restored Mrs. Swisshelm finished the reading of her address and began to extemporize. "A hushed attention fell upon the audience, inside and out. Then there was applause inside, which called forth howls from the outside, and when I stepped from the platform, I was overwhelmed with congratulations, and more astonished than any one, to learn that I could speak in public."

The meeting voted—and that vote should be recorded among the tales of frontier justice—that a press and type should be purchased so that Mrs. Swisshelm might publish a newspaper with whose editorial policy most of the subscribers knew they would disagree.

When the excitement was over and she was safe at home again Jane Swisshelm had a nervous collapse, so serious—she never did anything by halves—that for many days her life was despaired of. But she rallied pluckily and by May 13 the *Visiter* had resumed publication.

In the meantime Lowry and Shepley had been trying to explain to the public that their conduct had been actuated by no political motives, only by their desire to protect the reputation of a woman. But this version did not carry much weight. The report of the Stearns House meeting had gone out to the newspapers of the territory, had spread across the nation, and was proving effective Republican ammunition. Mrs. Swisshelm did not let the matter drop. She reverted to it again and again and even reprinted the editorial which had been the cause of the attack.

Finally Shepley could stand it no longer. He brought a $10,000 libel suit against the *Visiter* and the men who had helped to re-establish it. His terms of compromise were the publication in the *Visiter* of a "card" giving his version of the controversy and an agreement by Mrs.

Swisshelm, under bond, never again to refer to the affair in her pages. To the surprise of her backers she agreed. They could not, she knew, afford to defend the suit. "You sign that paper," she told them, "just as you would hand your money to a robber who held a pistol to your head."

On July 29 the *Visiter* carried the required statement by Shepley. On August 5 no *Visiter* appeared—but St. Cloud read a new paper, the *Democrat*, Jane G. Swisshelm sole editor and proprietor. The death of the *Visiter* was announced in a column heavily bordered with black and this was followed by a complete history of the Lowry-Shepley quarrel. "We have pledged *our* honor," wrote the editor and proprietor, "that the paper we edit will discuss any subject we have a mind. . . . If these fellows destroy our office again, as they now threaten to do, we will go down to Hennepin County; and publish the St. Cloud *Democrat* there."

The opposition succumbed. Mrs. Swisshelm was never seriously troubled again. She said what she had a mind to in the columns of her Republican *Democrat*. (She thought the word Democrat too good to be the property of a single party.) Shepley and Palmer she never forgave but her attitude towards General Lowry changed to pity when he suddenly became insane and was taken to a private sanitarium. During his periods of lucidity he corresponded with Mrs. Swisshelm, addressing her with friendship and admiration.

Though she continued to assert that she was not a Republican, Jane Swisshelm did such yeoman service for the cause that during the pre-election campaign of 1859 the Moccasin Democrats in St. Cloud burned her in effigy as "the mother of the Republican party." Her response was characteristic: "If you should take us, instead of a straw figure, and burn us we would talk to you all the time—talk to you, so that you would never cease to hear it the longest day of your lives."

Seward was Mrs. Swisshelm's candidate for president in 1860. She greeted the nomination of Lincoln without enthusiasm though admitting that it was probably the best the party could do under the circumstances. She worked for his election but through most of his administration was skeptical of his policies. Either moderation or compromise she found it difficult to understand.

At the same time that she won the right to print what she pleased Jane Swisshelm discovered that she could increase her influence by pleading her cause in person as well as on paper. On that evening when she addressed the crowd in the Stearns House parlors she found, what she would have known at thirteen had she been born in this generation, that she was an effective public speaker. And she had come far enough now from her literal interpretation of the Bible to feel it no sin but rather a divine command to use this "talent hidden in a napkin." The talent included a pleasant voice, a swift wit, an easy flow of language, and that surplus vitality which American audiences drink up so avidly, seeking from their orators a renewing of energy rather than a repointing of mind.

When, therefore, she was invited to make the address at one of a series of anti-slavery meetings in St. Anthony, Mrs. Swisshelm promptly accepted. She spoke in St. Anthony on November 15, 1858, and repeated her address the next evening in Minneapolis, both times to crowded houses. Her reputation as a speaker swiftly grew. A lecture tour of Minnesota became part of her annual schedule and often she went farther afield. She had a variety of subjects but her favorites were "Woman and Politics" and "Slavery as I Have Seen It in a Slave State." The Politics lecture "gave an account of the wrongs heaped upon woman by slavery, as a reason why women were then called upon for special activity."

Horace Mann had warned women to stand back, saying: "Politics is a stygian pool." I insisted that politics had reached this condition through the permit given to Satan to turn all the waste water of his mills into this pool; that this grant must be rescinded and the pool drained at all hazards. Indeed the emergency was such that even women might handle shovels.

During the editor's absence the *Democrat* was conducted by her nephew William B. Mitchell and in letters addressed to him she gave her readers lively accounts of her journeyings. She described the growing cities of Minnesota, its developing agriculture and industry, the state of travel, the leading citizens, usually her hosts, in each community where she lectured. They are good gossipy letters, full of information and shrewd comment, using personal experience to illustrate and illuminate ideas in the best manner of the twentieth-century columnist.

In one of her early letters Mrs. Swisshelm set forth the logic of her conversion to the lecture platform:

We have not lightly or irreverently set aside the injunction of Paul "Let women keep silence in churches"; but mature reflection and comparison of this passage with other passages of Scripture, and with the universal usage of all Christian churches convinces us that this is one of the passages Paul wrote "by permission, not by command."

In all branches of the Christian Church, except the Friends, women are expected to sing as loud as they are able; and this is certainly as far from "keeping silence" as any talking could ever be. Anna, a prophetess, "Spake of the child Jesus, to all them that looked for Redemption in Israel." It must have been in the Temple she spake, for she *departed not from it;* and as it was women who were first sent to proclaim a risen Savior, we maintain that our sex does not disqualify us for delivering any message we may feel the Lord has sent by us; and that it is no profanation of the walls of a church to reverberate to the sound of a woman's voice.

The lecture tours continued even after the outbreak of the Civil War. Mrs. Swisshelm was at first bitterly opposed to the taking up of arms against the South—if they want to secede, let them go—but, once convinced that war was inevitable, she supported it with all her energies, with words and with deeds.

When the First Minnesota Regiment was organized she proposed that the ladies of the community supply the St. Cloud volunteers with socks, towels, blankets, soap, and sewing kits and, finding no one ready to undertake the direction of the work, she did it herself. She formed a society of which she was "President, Vice President, Secretary, Treasurer, Manager and all the members"; she solicited goods from the merchants of St. Cloud and per-suaded the ladies of the Baptist Sewing Circle to make them up into hospital supplies.

She visited the Regiment at Fort Snelling, near Minne-apolis, where they were stationed before their departure for the front, and gave her readers a detailed account of their condition and way of life. Curious about everything, bombarding officers and men alike with questions, practical and ideological, she satisfied herself that the troops understood the cause for which they were fighting while she inspected with a housekeeper's eye their bedding, equipment, uniforms, and food. "We can see no reason," she wrote, "why soldiers should eat beans from the first of January to the last of December every year"—and she outlined a practicable diet, augmented by fruit and vegetables, which closely resembles our present army fare.

The withdrawal of the regular soldiers who had been garrisoning the forts and the departure of the volunteers left the thinly settled sections of Minnesota in grave peril from the Indians. Late in the summer the Sioux revolted and massacred hundreds of the white settlers. Murders were done within a few miles of St. Cloud and for weeks its citizens were in constant fear lest the Chippewa, who dwelt close by them, should rise also. Refugees kept coming in to the *Democrat* office with tales of horror and Mrs. Swisshelm issued daily bulletins giving what news could be had about the movements of the Indians. Families from the outskirts came into the town for protection and she had forty-two women and children camping in her house for weeks. "We kept large kettles of boiling water as one means of defense. I always had the watchword, and often at midnight I would go out to see that the pickets were on duty, and report to the women that all was well."

Minnesota citizens, aided by volunteers from Iowa and Wisconsin, finally succeeded in capturing a large number of Sioux, tried them for murder, and hanged thirty-eight, when the Federal Government intervened and took the prisoners out of their hands.

Missionaries and other clergymen aroused a good deal

of sympathy in the East for the poor Indian who was supposed to have been driven to his cruelties by the injustice
and ill-treatment of the whites. This attitude on the part
of those who had suffered no danger aroused Mrs. Swisshelm's indignation. The romantic admiration for the
Indian with which she had come West had completely
disappeared. She saw him now realistically, as a lazy, dirty
savage cunningly taking advantage of the white man who
pampered him because his occupation of the Indians' land
gave him a bad conscience. Our whole Indian policy appeared to her as a system "never equalled on earth for
crime committed with the best intentions. It intends to be
especially just, by holding that the Creator made North
America for the exclusive use of savages, and that civilization can only exist here by suffrance of the proprietors."
In addition to this, with her usual readiness to believe any
evil of the slavocracy, she was convinced that the Minnesota massacres had been instigated by the South. She
readily, therefore, agreed to the proposal that she undertake a speaking tour to enlighten the East on the attitude
of the frontier and that she go to Washington and attempt
to present the anti-Indian case to the President.

In January, 1863 she set out, spoke to large audiences
in Chicago, Philadelphia, Brooklyn, and Washington and
succeeded in making converts but was unable to obtain an
interview with the President who, she was assured, "will
hang nobody!"

She did meet Lincoln at a White House reception
where she studied him with her portrait painter's eye as
he shook hands with the crowd and found "his sad,
earnest, honest face . . . irresistible in its plea for confidence." She had more respect for his policies in the future.

Mr. Lincoln [she wrote] stood going through one of those dreadful ordeals of hand-shaking, working like a man pumping for life on a sinking vessel, and I was filled with indignation for the selfish people who made this useless drain on his nervous force. I wanted to stand between him and them, and say, "stand back, and let him live and do his work." But I could not resist going to him with the rest of the crowd, and when he took my hand I said:

"May the Lord have mercy on you, poor man, for the people have none."

He laughed heartily, and the men around him joined in his merriment. When I came to Mrs. Lincoln, she did not catch the name at first, and asked to hear it again, then repeated it, and a sudden glow of pleasure lit her face, as she held out her hand and said how very glad she was to see me. I objected to giving her my hand because my black glove would soil her white one; but she said:

"Then I shall preserve the glove to remember a great pleasure, for I have long wished to see you."

My escort was more surprised than I by her unusual cordiality, and said afterwards:

"It was no polite affectation. I cannot understand it from her."

I understood at once that I had met one with whom I was in sympathy. . . . and I recognized Mrs. Lincoln as a loyal, liberty-loving woman, more staunch even than her husband in opposition to the Rebellion and its cause, and as my very dear friend for life.

This swift attachment was genuine; the friendship continued into their old age when it was to see Mrs. Lincoln as much as her married daughter that Mrs. Swisshelm made journeys to Chicago.

Though she went to Washington as the agent for a cause, the most important result of Jane Swisshelm's visit was the change it made in her personal life. Soon after her arrival she encountered Secretary Stanton who recalled immediately their meeting in Pittsburgh and his admiration for her advocacy of the married woman's property act. He offered her an appointment as a clerk in the War Department; the government was trying the revolutionary experiment of employing women. Mrs. Swisshelm accepted at once. It meant a stable salary, $50 a month, far larger than anything she had ever made by her editing; it was pioneer work from the woman's rights point of view; and she would be working for the Union cause. As soon as the position was assured she sold the *Democrat* to her nephew and assistant editor William Mitchell.

While she waited for a desk to be ready for her in the Quartermaster's Office—appointments preceded vacancies—Mrs. Swisshelm tried to find work in the Washington hospitals which were crowded with wounded. She spent one day with an acquaintance who went from hospital to hospital delivering tracts but this did not seem to her a highly useful form of relief. An attempt to get some straw for the bed of a wretched patient whom she saw on this trip led her into quagmires of official procedure and medical etiquette where she floundered angry and helpless.

One of the quagmires was Dorothea Dix who at the outbreak of hostilities had offered her experience to the Union Government and had been appointed superintendent of all women nurses in military hospitals. To her Jane Swisshelm, like many other people, took at first meeting a violent dislike, which was apparently returned, for Miss Dix declined to accept her as one of her nurses.

The Sanitary Commission Mrs. Swisshelm found efficient but cold, and they had all the workers they needed. When she went with some ladies to visit friends of theirs who were patients in Campbell Hospital she again tendered her services and was again told that there was nothing she could do. This time she believed it for Campbell was a first-class hospital well staffed and run, so she was speaking perfunctorily when she asked a Wisconsin man in one of the wards whether there was anything she could do for him. He replied rather timidly that he wished she could bring him "something to quench thirst. . . . it gets very warm in here in the afternoons and we cannot get out in the shade. We drink so much water it does not agree with us and if we had something sour to drink or some kind of fruit it would taste very good!"

Here was work. Next morning Jane Swisshelm wrote a note to the New York *Tribune* relating the incident and stating her determination to spend the afternoons in giving cooling drinks to the wounded if she could get the necessary supplies. She bought lemons and sugar and went to the hospital at noon, taking the lemonade from bed to bed. She tried carefully as she went about not to disturb the male nurses for she knew that women attendants were rigidly excluded from Campbell and she expected at any moment to be ordered off.

When about done, I came into the ward where Mr. Snare lay. The nurses were dressing his thigh stump; and he was in an extremity of agony. I felt that the man who held the stump held it badly and setting down pitcher and glass I went and placing my hands on each side of his held it up and asked him to remove his hands. He did so and the agonizing groan of the patient stopped instantly. I asked him if I held it easier, and he replied so earnestly:

"Oh yes, oh yes!"

"Then, I shall always hold it up for you while they dress it!"

"You could not. It would be too much trouble," was the sad, despairing answer.

"But I *can* a great deal easier than not, for I have not anything in the world to do."

"Oh if you could, but you won't be here!"

"I'll come."

I held up the other stump while it was dressed and the nurse, who was a very superior one, said "how easily and tenderly you hold it!"

To me this was a voice from God. I had never, during the whole course of my life, helped dress a dangerous wound; and if I could so lessen the pain it was a divine commission.

She did come back next day, and sat by the deathbed of her first patient. Then she found more wounds to dress and other services to render, and while she worked she made a conscious effort to keep up a running flow of amusing talk because she saw that it pleased and distracted the patients. She was entirely unaware that she had been the day before under observation by the surgeon in chief, Dr. Baxter, and was completely taken by surprise when, towards the end of the afternoon, he sent to offer her a room if she cared to stay and work in the hospital. This was contrary to all his own regulations for he had declined to have any women nurses at Campbell, not liking those selected by Miss Dix. Mrs. Swisshelm accepted at once and went into residence as the only woman in a community of some two thousand males.

The account of her hospital nursing, which lasted only

Ward in a Union hospital such as Mrs. Swisshelm nursed in, drawn by Thomas Nast

a matter of months, occupies more than a quarter of Jane Swisshelm's autobiography. It was the part of her life which she most cared to dwell upon, to recall in detail. She lived during those months with the heightened intensity which war gives to all experience; she was proud that she could do work for which few of her sex were fitted—most of the ladies and the Sisters of Charity who worked in the hospitals concerned themselves with the distribution of foods and comforts, not with the dressing of wounds; but there were other reasons beyond these.

That period of nursing was the only time in Jane Swisshelm's life when she worked in an atmosphere of approval, continually expressed. No relatives criticized her doings and lamented them, no newspapers bombarded her with angry paragraphs; to have encouragement, not opposition in well-doing was restful and very sweet. It was new to her also, and pleasant, to measure the results of her work in concrete terms. It is so difficult to be certain of the results of propaganda that it seems often an unrewarding trade but when the wounded man whose bleeding leg-stump you are holding ceases to groan or the fever patient falls into a quiet sleep you can know that your work has been right. The chief pleasure, though, which Jane Swisshelm found in her hospital work was the use it made of all her powers. The knowledge of anatomy which she called "instinctive" derived from her habit of looking at people with a portrait painter's eye, desiring to draw each face and figure, considering the flex of a muscle in back or shoulder, the center of balance as the subject sat or moved, the relative position, in a multitude of poses, of hands and feet. She did not know the names of bones and muscles but she knew their functions. And her painter's hands, those long thin fingers so quick at making lace or tracing flowers on velvet, found now, for the first time since they foreswore the paintbrush, a labor which required their utmost dexterity, a dexterity guided by sympathy and intelligence to an end that was indubitably good.

In the course of her long account of those hospital days Mrs. Swisshelm recorded two explanations of her conduct made to her by two very different men. Since she sets them both down without comment we may take it, I think, that both were true.

One remark was made by General Lowry in a curious friendly talk they had together shortly before his death. He had been released from the asylum at the moment, in September, 1863, when Mrs. Swisshelm was given a brief leave of absence from the Quartermaster's Department to go to Minnesota, sell the *Democrat*, and close her house. General Lowry called upon her and they spent an hour in talk, chiefly about the war. She was impressed, as she had been in the past, by "the genuine greatness of the man, who had been degraded by the use of irresponsible power."

I tried to avoid all personal matters, as well as reference to our quarrel, but he broke into the conversation to say:

"I am the only person who ever understood you. People now think you go into hospitals from a sense of duty; from benevolence, like those good people who expect to get to heaven by doing disagreeable things on earth; but I know you go because you must; go for your own pleasure; you do not care for heaven or anything else, but yourself."

He stopped, looked down, traced the pattern of the carpet with the point of his cane, then raised his head and continued: "You take care of the sick and wounded, go into all those dreadful places just as I used to drink brandy—for the sake of the exhilaration it brings you."

The other explanation of her conduct was given Mrs. Swisshelm by a fever patient whose name she never knew: "Good many ladies has been kind to us, but none uv 'em ever loved us but you! . . . we know 'at you don't take care uv us 'cause it's your juty! you jist do it 'cause you love to!"

On the first day of her service at Campbell Mrs. Swisshelm had discovered the need for lemons, not merely to quench thirst but to prevent what was known as hospital gangrene. Horrified at the half box apportioned by the Sanitary Commission to seven hundred and fifty patients, she dashed off a note to the New York *Tribune:*

Hospital gangrene has broken out in Washington, and we want lemons! *lemons!* LEMONS! LEMONS! No man or woman in health, has a right to a glass of lemonade until these men have all they need; send us lemons!

Lemons and money poured into Washington in response. "At one time there were twenty ladies, several of them with ambulances, distributing those which came to my address."

How well she could adapt herself to a system when that seemed more efficacious than fighting it, this portion of Jane Swisshelm's autobiography shows. She had found work which it seemed to her imperative to perform and she saw that she could do it only if she made herself acceptable to those in authority. She proceeded with modesty and tact. She was careful not to impose on anyone, careful to ask assistance always as a favor, careful to undertake no work in any ward without the permission of the surgeon in charge. Her critical observations she kept to herself and she took pains to be friendly and amusing to the staff as well as to her patients so that she succeeded in inspiring both gratitude and affection.

She was usually addressed as "Mother," after it had been established that she was not a Sister of Charity. The plain straight dress she wore caused her to be asked continually to what order she belonged, a question to which she responded tartly that she belonged exclusively to herself. She had no love for the Catholic Church. Still less did she love the fine ladies who, coming to visit in the hospital or staying to nurse sons and brothers, yet declined to put off their hoops and furbelows and dress appropriately for the work. The autobiography contains a horror tale of an elegant damsel who caused a fatal hemorrhage when she caught her hoop on the bedstead of an amputation case.

Though she suffered acutely from these stupidities and others on the part of the staff, only once in the course of her nursing did Jane Swisshelm revert to her usual method of reform. This was when she had been asked by a friend to visit her brother, lying wounded in Douglas Hospital. Douglas was known as a "model" institution, a term which always roused Mrs. Swisshelm's suspicion; a model institution was likely to put emphasis on nonessentials. She was not completely surprised, therefore, though thoroughly horrified to find that under immaculate white counterpanes on geometrically made beds were blankets crawling with lice and that most of the patients had not been washed since they were brought in from the battlefield.

Her earlier experience with army bureaucracy discouraged her from reporting her findings to any of the responsible officials. Instead she took up her pen again and sent a letter to the *Tribune*. Unfortunately she dated it from Campbell Hospital and official wrath descended. Dr. Baxter was ordered to dismiss her.

Unwilling to lose her services he suggested that she appeal in person to the Surgeon General, so, she writes:

I . . . saw the man who held the lives of my patients in his hands, ate the only piece of humble pie that ever crossed my lips, by apologizing for telling the truth, and got permission to go back to the men who looked to me for life.

I have felt that I made a great mistake—felt that if I had then and there made war to the knife, and the knife to the hilt, against the whole system of fraud and cruelty embodied in the hospital service, I should have saved many more lives in the end.

The humble pie served only temporarily for the *Tribune* letter brought her irregular position in Campbell to the attention of Miss Dix and other persons in authority and Dr. Baxter was so bombarded by requests for her dismissal that when the special cases in her charge were cured he let her go.

Mrs. Swisshelm had been so absorbed in her work in the hospital that she had not heeded a summons to begin her service in the War Department and so had lost her place, but Secretary Stanton reinstated her and after she left Campbell she began her clerkship. Six hours a day spent sitting down seemed to her at first no work at all but she found that it was not possible to copy documents for any longer period without beginning to make serious mistakes.

The newspaper readers who had been stirred by her letters to the *Tribune* and *Democrat* continued to send fruit and other delicacies for the wounded and until the end of the war Mrs. Swisshelm kept a number of ladies busy distributing them. She herself shared the work whenever her hours permitted. In 1864, at the time of the Battle of the Wilderness, she asked permission to go to Fredericksburg and for days there was in charge of an old theater filled with badly wounded men who lay packed together on the floor without even blankets to cover them. Her nursing skill, her energy, and ingenuity were all called into play and for days she performed heroic labors.

The work in the Quartermaster's Office was far more ladylike and peaceful than the labor she performed in the hospitals but here again Mrs. Swisshelm was a pioneer. "This advance post," she called her desk, "on the picket line of civilization," for the nation was watching with apprehension the Washington bureaus which were trying the dangerous experiment of employing women.

As a test of female ability the experiment was not precisely ideal. There were as yet no civil service examinations; appointments were made by influence, like Mrs. Swisshelm's own, and Members of Congress found in the new practice a convenient way of providing for indigent female relatives, of providing also for females whose relationship to them would not always bear inspection, a situation which Mrs. Swisshelm did not hesitate to call to the attention of the public.

On November 13, 1865, she wrote a long letter to the *Democrat* urging voters to take cognizance of the important social experiment that was being tried and to see that it was not abandoned, as it seemed likely to be, on the wrong grounds. She made her points by a series of portraits, lively satirical portraits, of her sister clerks.

Another comes sailing in at 9½ o'clock, gets off her wraps; sinks into her chair with the air of a willow wand cracked in the middle; languidly asks some one to call a servant; sends said servant, with her compliments, to the head of the bureau for the loan of his morning paper; reads it leisurely, with a running comment, loud enough to be heard all over that room and in the one adjoining, on the houses to rent, the late appointments and removals; tells who built the house for sale on such a street and who lived in it at such a time; gives an inventory of their furniture and history of their family in its lateral and collateral branches; finds who is dead and who married, and does as much for their geneological trees; begins writing at 10½, but keeps up the stream of small talk until some other lady is through with her morning paper; when she reads that, gets several new texts, and goes on with the commentary until 2 or 2½ o'clock, when, being quite worn out with her day's labor, she gracefully retires.

Pictures of other types follow and then a description of the "majority of female clerks with whose dullness and demeanor it would be difficult to find fault—women working like horses, scarcely taking time for lunch, making books of records second to none, and copies of important papers with wonderful rapidity and correctness; . . . At the end of the month all get equal pay. Their chances of promotion are the same, and special favors are for those who have done the least work. What wonder that the experiment is thought by many to be a failure?"

This was the sort of battle for woman's rights which Jane Swisshelm thought it expedient to win before asking for the ballot.

When President Johnson began his administration Mrs. Swisshelm thought his policy correct and admirable but as he became more conciliatory towards the South she turned violently against him. She believed that the guilty—slaveholders or Indians—should suffer and Johnson's clemency seemed to her nothing less than treachery. When an anti-administration group in the capital began to feel the need of an organ Mrs. Swisshelm agreed to edit the *Reconstructionist* which started its existence on December 21, 1865. Its tone was violent and its life was brief.

One can scarcely blame the President for taking exception to an editorial which stated: "That he was prepared beforehand to serve the purposes of treason there can be no doubt; that his administration and its programme were part and parcel of the assassination plot, we have no longer the shadow of a doubt." The accusation was mitigated by the admission that Johnson probably did not know of the assassination plot beforehand, but the President saw no reason why a government employee should be accusing him of treason. He ordered Mrs. Swisshelm's dismissal, "the first person dismissed by Mr. Johnson," she records proudly in the autobiography.

She did not fight the decree; perhaps she was weary, more probably she felt that this was not, like abolition, a cause for which to die. She submitted quietly and resigned herself to the prospect of a life of poverty, for she was fifty years old and had no other income than her salary.

Just at that moment she learned that she had a claim on part of the Swisshelm estate in Swissvale. On Secretary Stanton's advice she prosecuted and won. Then, in the old log blockhouse, "rescued from the tooth of decay," Jane Swisshelm of the *Visiter*, the *Democrat*, and the *Reconstructionist* settled down to the peace of which she had so often dreamed.

It was only a partial peace, though. Whenever, within her narrowed range of observation or her wider range of newspaper reading, she noted an incident which could be moulded into shot for her anti-Catholic, anti-Indian, or pro-woman's rights campaigns, she caught up her pen again and dashed off a pungent column which she sent, most often, to the New York *Independent*. And in 1880, just four years before she died, she brought all her causes together in that vigorous autobiography *Half a Century*.

Amelia Bloomer, from the *Lily*,
September, 1851

The Lily and the Bloomer

AMELIA BLOOMER

Bloomer is a word that it is difficult to pronounce without a smile. The b and double o conjure up inevitably, by a sort of visual onomatopoeia, the puffed "trousers," of silk or serge, that once so shocked our nation. A better noun for them could not have been invented than the name of the lady who is so largely responsible for modern woman's comfortable dress.

The laughter that has pursued Amelia Bloomer for a hundred years has almost obscured her fame, but that would not disturb her. Ridicule she took always with the charming good temper that was one of her best assets as a reformer. Through laughter or abuse she went quietly on with her work. She never answered slander with slander, not even with anger, but neither did she give way before it; she met it with facts and common sense. For personal prestige she did not care; what she wanted was to bring America nearer to perfection. Dress reform, to her mind, was useful but only a corollary to more important freedoms. "The emancipation of Woman from Intemperance, Injustice, Prejudice and Bigotry": that was the high purpose she announced on the masthead of the little Seneca Falls newspaper that made the bloomer famous.

Amelia Jenks, who became The Bloomer, was born May 27, 1818, in the town of Homer in Cortland County, New York. Her parents were good Presbyterians who instilled in her a sense of duty and of obligation. She expected to do her share of work in the world and she thought it incumbent upon her to attempt a cure for those ills of society she was clear headed enough to diagnose.

Ananias Jenks, Amelia's father, was a clothier in good though far from affluent circumstances. She had three elder sisters and two brothers, one of whom, Augustus, died at Gettysburg. Her education was of the simplest: a few terms at the district school where she learned reading, writing, and arithmetic; and a thorough training in the domestic arts. She had "faculty" in the kitchen and she was quick at her book but she was not very far above the average in either line. That is one of the most interesting things about her. From the neighbors with whom she worked in church guilds and village temperance societies she differed only in the clarity of her thinking and the vigor with which she acted on her beliefs. She is an admirable text for a sermon on the two talents. She points, in fact, so good a moral that she is scarcely an appropriate subject for twentieth-century biography.

At seventeen Amelia began to earn her living. She taught a term in a school near Clyde and then her sister Elvira, who was married and living in Waterloo, found a place for her as governess to the three small children of a Mr. Oren Chamberlain.

Waterloo was an important station in Amelia's life. It

was there that she met a tall, slim young man "of bashful and reserved demeanor"—the phrase is his own—who was studying law, was interested in politics, and was one of the editors and proprietors of the only Whig paper in the county, the Seneca County *Courier*. "Friendship ripened into love," to quote again from Dexter Bloomer's biography of his wife, a biography of bashful demeanor but quite definite charm and many lawyer's virtues. It is judicious, meticulous, minute, and accurate. It has also, unfortunately, the virtue of conciseness.

At the time of their marriage, Dexter Bloomer tells us, Amelia was "five feet four inches in height, and weighed about a hundred pounds. She had a well-formed head, bright, blue eyes, bordering on black, auburn hair and an exceedingly pleasant and winning smile." After this accurate detail one accepts unquestioningly his comments on his wife's character, that she was "reserved in manner, and very unwilling to force herself upon the notice of strangers, but when she once became acquainted with them she enjoyed their society most heartily"; that her "kindness of heart" was united with "wonderful firmness and a strict regard for truth and right"; that she had "strong perceptive faculties and noticed what she believed to be the mistakes and failings of others, perhaps, too freely." To illustrate Amelia's character further her husband tells a little story of their wedding breakfast.

The marriage took place on April 15, 1840, and, at the request of the "advanced" young couple, the clergyman omitted from the service the word "obey." After the ceremony the bride and groom went to Seneca Falls, where they were to board for the first few months with Dexter Bloomer's publishing partner and his wife. When they

arrived they found the Fullers' parlors filled with friends
who had come to welcome them to their new home. The
fire company of "able and respectable" men, to which
Mr. Bloomer belonged, had brought their band and the
party was gay. The refreshments included "a plentiful
supply of wine, for in those days, this was the almost certain accompaniment of all social gatherings." Glasses were
filled and one of them was presented by the bridegroom
to the "young and happy bride." She firmly yet pleasantly declined to accept it.

"What," he said with the greatest earnestness, "will you not
drink a glass of wine with me on this joyful occasion? Surely
it can do you no harm." "No," she smilingly yet firmly replied, "I cannot,—I must not." A crowd of guests standing
around could but admire her great self-denial and devotion
to principles; and ever after, to the end of her days, she was
the firm and consistent advocate of Temperance and the un-
ceasing enemy of strong drink in all its varied forms.

It is a significant little story, as its teller was aware. No
social pressure, no "what will the neighbors think," not
even love ever deflected Amelia Bloomer from the path
that she saw to be right. She had complete personal integrity, but she had no conceit. She was so quiet and good-
tempered about her principles that you could never be
annoyed or write her down a prig. You were practically
sure to like her even when you thought she went too far.

During their courtship Dexter Bloomer's editorial eye
had been struck by the excellence of Amelia's letters.
After their marriage he persuaded her to try her hand at
newspaper articles. She was reluctant to believe that she
had ability but compliant enough to experiment and soon
the local papers were carrying little paragraphs of hers,

signed of course with pseudonyms. "Gloriana" was her favorite.

Unlike most of her contemporaries, Gloriana did not begin her literary apprenticeship with nature rhapsodies or paragraphs of domestic chat; she began with propaganda. Even in her teens Amelia had begun to wrestle independently with moral and intellectual problems. At twenty-two she found herself with reasons for the faith that was in her; she had ideas of her own on temperance and religion, on politics and that explosive new issue, the position of women. In her modest conviction that she had no great literary gift she was perfectly accurate. Her writing is neither racy, elegant, nor particularly original but it was read, and is readable today, because she wrote on subjects which thoroughly interested her and on which she had something definite to say. Dexter Bloomer's impression of her journalistic ability was sound.

While the literary experiment went on Mrs. Bloomer was taking her place in the community. Seneca Falls in 1840 was a charming and thriving village. Lying at the head of Seneca, the largest of the Finger Lakes, it was already making good use of its strategic location and its excellent water power, building the mills that were to become famous for their pumps and window sashes and threshing machines. It was building, too, the ample well-proportioned houses with correctly ordered white columns which make it still a pleasant place to live. The broad streets are tree-lined; the air is fresh and light, a good air to work in, with your brains or with your hands. It may be more than coincidence that so many strong-minded women, so many men who labored for a better world flourished in central New York.

Mrs. Bloomer tried her hand at political reform by help-ing the local Whigs during the Harrison-Tyler campaign. She took an active part in church affairs—she and her hus-band, whose parents were Quakers, joined the Episcopal church, finding there, as Catharine Beecher did, a God less terrible and more loving than the deity under whom they had been brought up; and she continued her interest in the temperance movement. When the Seneca Falls Ladies' Temperance Society was formed in 1848, Mrs. Bloomer was made vice president.

To anyone who has lived through the horrors of Pro-hibition the nineteenth-century zeal for temperance seems often funny and almost always exaggerated, yet temper-ance in the decades before the Civil War was a progressive and a very necessary reform. From the time of the Rev-olution on America had become increasingly a nation of drunkards. The brewing of beer and the making of wine were so difficult for the unskilled, unequipped pioneer that the habit developed of drinking rum, easily export-able from the West Indies, and whiskey which could be made on almost any farm. It was the accepted belief that daily drams were a dietary necessity for any man doing heavy physical labor. No employer could hire workmen unless he promised them wages in hard liquor as well as cash. Heavy drinking went on as a matter of course at all social gatherings and at professional meetings of all kinds, even meetings of the clergy, as Lyman Beecher eloquently testified. The drunkard's wife who appears so frequently in nineteenth-century fiction appeared all too frequently in nineteenth-century fact. Some change in the national habit, in the attitude of the average man and woman towards drink, was seriously needed. The temperance cause enlisted workers on social as well as moral and religious grounds.

The ladies of the Seneca Falls Temperance Society, glowing with new enthusiasm, projected the publication of a temperance journal. Not till they had issued a prospectus and taken in some money for subscriptions did they pause to consider the pitfalls and dangers of newspaper editing. Then they grew frightened and decided to cancel the whole plan. Vice President Bloomer was distressed. Her vigorous common sense, never blurred by timidity, marked the deeper implications of retreat. The Society, she held, was responsible for its promises to subscribers, and besides people would say that to start such a scheme and then abandon it was "just like women," "what more could you expect of them?" Mrs. Bloomer felt it incumbent upon her to uphold the reputation of her sex as well as the temperance cause; she offered to edit the *Lily* herself. (The paper's name had been suggested by the president of the Society and the members thought it pretty as well as symbolical, more delicately feminine than the local Washingtonian Society's *Water Bucket*. Amelia Bloomer was too good a democrat not to accept the majority's voice but she admitted later that she never liked the name.)

Her editorial adventure Mrs. Bloomer undertook with much inward trepidation. She was one of the first women in the country to dare such a deed as publishing a journal and though her project was less hazardous than Mrs. Swisshelm's—temperance was a far more ladylike cause than abolition—the people who admired her course were few compared to those who condemned. She did not know very much either of the technical side of newspaper editing but she felt she could learn. She did know what she wanted the *Lily* to do. It was to be devoted, her masthead announced, to Temperance and Literature, because "chastening in its influence—ennobling the mind—expanding the intellect with knowledge—a beautiful and appropriate hand maid is given to Temperance by this association."

The subscription price of the *Lily* was 50¢ a year. Mrs. Bloomer had no funds with which to pay contributors but by skillful selection and solicitation, and by writing large sections of the paper herself, she managed to produce a well-balanced, interesting little journal, eight three-column pages each month.

The hand maid furnished for each issue a "selected tale" which, in its ability to make you read it against your better judgment, is closely allied to the moral advertising story of today. Each has a heroine in a quandary and their problems are similar: how can He be induced to ask Her hand in marriage? or, if She is already married, what must She do to retain Her Husband's Love? For the twentieth century the answer is easy: use Rinso, Lifebuoy, or Listerine; but a hundred years ago success was not so neatly packaged. The *Lily's* readers were instructed to attain their ends by employing sweet temper, careful household economy, or kindness to the poor.

Not all the story writers were directly concerned with temperance but the poets were invariably and to them the easy symbolism of the *Lily's* name was a great boon. Clear water in a crystal cup was offered month after month by lilies to young men with fevered brows. Sometimes Mrs. Bloomer grew impatient with these platitudinous poetasters. "It has some good points," she would remark of a poem "respectfully declined," "but we think the writer would hardly like to see it in print. She would probably do better at writing prose."

Not all the contributors were zealous amateurs. Professional writers concerned for the cause were glad to encourage the new organ by offering matter for its pages. One of the early numbers contains a poem by John Greenleaf Whittier, which is introduced as having "just beamed down upon us from one of the *fixed stars*."

As the *Lily* grew and prospered Mrs. Bloomer felt freer to use her editorial discrimination. She did not hesitate to reject unsatisfactory contributions, however lofty their purpose, checking them off with sharp little notes in the monthly column through which she answered all her correspondence. The tone is not unlike that of a schoolmistress correcting themes.

"De Forest"—we must decline your article. You need much practice before you write for the public. You spell badly— make use of capital letters where there should be none, and omit them where they should be used. Other errors might be pointed out, but these will suffice. We cannot give it an insertion in its present state, and have no time to re-write it.

We wish to deal in all fairness with our correspondents, and instead of discouraging, would encourage and aid them, in their endeavors to cultivate a taste for writing and composition; and we cordially invite all to contribute to our columns. —Some articles may be refused—probably will, but the writing of them, by calling the thoughts into action, may be a benefit to the writers, and practice may result in perfection.

The most interesting parts of the paper are those Amelia Bloomer wrote herself: most of the editorials, rejoinders to reprinted articles or correspondence, and bits of temperance news. Some of these are stern and horrifying little items set down effectively without comment:

A man when drunk fell into a kettle of boiling brine at Liverpool, Onondaga co., and was scalded to death.

A young man named Dow, while intoxicated, cut the throat of his wife, at Seabrook, N.H., on Friday last.

Catharine Mann, an intemperate woman, was frozen to death in Newark, N.J., on Tuesday night.

Amelia Bloomer came by degrees to the conviction that literature and moral suasion were not enough, that the nation could be made temperate only by legislation; but before she reached that point of view she printed many columns of editorial exhortation. A generation nourished on pulpit oratory had an almost insatiable appetite for the rolling periods that put a twentieth-century reader quietly to sleep, and Mrs. Bloomer's ability in this kind was admired. Far more effective, to the modern taste, are the straightforward courageous attacks she made upon intemperance as she saw it in Seneca Falls, taking local errors as texts for her general sermons.

February, 1849
It is with feelings of surprise and regret, that we hear that there are ladies in our village who can deliberately fill the intoxicating cup for their friends who call on New Years day. . . . this small number are of a class whose influence is felt for good, or for evil, and when arrayed on the side of evil much injury may be done, though their number be small.

That paragraph set the little village by the ears but Mrs. Bloomer did not budge from her position.

Our remarks [she wrote in the next issue] were not made with reference to our own village alone, but were intended for all to whom they might apply. It seems, however, that the coat set so closely in some quarters as to cause uneasiness, and we are censured for having got so good a fit.

We are happy to know that the ladies whom we had supposed to be the offending ones, are guiltless. The ones hit we had never thought of, and if they had kept their own counsel, we should never have been the wiser.

A few weeks later she upset her fellow townswomen again.

There is one pernicious practice existing among our own sex, which we feel bound to expose and condemn. It is the use of intoxicating liquors in culinary preparations. There are ladies who profess to think it impossible to prepare food fit for the palate, unless they mix with it a certain quantity of deleterious compound in the form of alcohol. These ladies stand greatly in the way of the temperance reform. While they may condemn the use of intoxicating liquors as a beverage, and pretend to be greatly in favor of temperance, yet they insist upon it, that cake, mince pie, or puddings, cannot be made eatable without it—and their friends must take just so much of the poison, as they see fit to season their food with.

In the same year in which she planted the militant *Lily* Mrs. Bloomer shattered another precedent. She became a postmaster. Her husband's services to the Whig party had been rewarded with the postmastership of Seneca Falls and he appointed her his deputy. She undertook the work, she said, because she was "determined to give a practical demonstration of woman's right to fill any place for which she had capacity," and she served, to the general satisfaction of the community, during the four years of the Taylor-Filmore administration. All the lions, as usual, lay down in her path. She demonstrated, as she had hoped to do, that a woman might engage in "any respectable business and deal with all sorts of men, and yet be treated with the utmost respect and consideration." Her neighbors, though, continued to shake their heads. How could any woman run both a newspaper and a postoffice without shamefully neglecting her husband's meals and socks? Mrs. Bloomer, who was perfectly ready to discuss her private affairs if she could thereby serve a principle, told them:

"I suppose you have a girl to do your house work?" "You are not your own house-keeper, Mrs. Bloomer?" "Why! you don't take care of your house, edit your paper, tend post office, and all?" *Yes, we do all this*, and have beside, *one* little prattler * under our care and protection; and we assure those who may have fears on the subject, that *she* does not suffer for want of food or clothing.

Since April last we have done the entire work of our house, in addition to our duties as clerk and publisher. We cannot say of how much more we are capable, but think we could manage one or two more children—provided they did not want much attention. True, we have not much time to read novels, study the fashions, or gossip with idlers; yet we find time to read many things useful, to study ourself, and to visit our friends.

Now friends, are you answered?

The ladies of Seneca Falls did approve the "neat little room" adjoining the postoffice which Mrs. Bloomer fitted up as a sort of woman's club where the *Lily's* contributors and subscribers could meet when they came to town for shopping and the mail. Temperance was discussed there and also women's rights, for other strong-minded hearts

* Mrs. Bloomer had no children of her own but she was always looking after at least one small niece or nephew.

besides that of the postmistress beat behind the Greek Revival pillars of Seneca Falls. The first woman's rights convention was called there in 1848 by Elizabeth Cady Stanton who, despite the opposition of her friends, insisted on asking not only for legal rights for women but for the ballot itself. Her revolutionary resolution was passed as an addendum to the convention's Declaration, a skillful feminist parody of the document of 1776.

Mrs. Bloomer attended that convention but she neither spoke nor signed the Declaration. She thought the suffrage question over long and carefully before she committed herself and began to work for the ballot. It is interesting to watch, in the *Lily's* columns, the steady, logical increase of her strong-mindedness. She was never swayed by emotion nor by what other people thought but she advanced month after month closer to the frontiers of woman's expanding sphere. Her mind did not move rapidly but it moved straight, and independently; she worked out all her principles for herself. The assumption that either she or the *Lily* was influenced by Mrs. Stanton always amused her. "Sunflower," as Mrs. Stanton signed herself in the *Lily's* columns, was a valued co-worker but not a guide.

Some of our gentlemen readers are a little troubled lest we should injure ourself and our paper by saying too much in behalf of the rights and interests of our own sex, and it has even been intimated to us that we are controlled in the matter by some person or persons. Now while we feel very thankful for the disinterested kindness of friends, we wish them to give themselves no uneasiness on our account, as we feel perfectly competent to manage our own affairs, and wish not to hold them responsible for our doings. We would here say distinctly that no one besides ourself has any control over the columns of the Lily and we know not that we are controlled in our actions by any one.

What Mrs. Stanton thought of Mrs. Bloomer we know from a confidential letter to Miss Anthony, published posthumously. It was written probably in 1851:

I think you are doing up the temperance business just right. But do not let the conservative element control. For instance, you must take Mrs. Bloomer's suggestions with great caution, for she has not the spirit of the true reformer. . . . In her paper she will not speak against the Fugitive Slave Law, nor in her work to put down intemperance will she criticize the equivocal position of the Church. She trusts to numbers to build up a cause rather than to principles, to the truth and the right. Fatal error! . . . All this I say to you and to no one else, and you will understand why. I would not speak aught to injure Mrs. Bloomer. Yet, I repeat, beware of her conservative suggestions.

That these women of such opposite temperaments could work together so long and so effectively is a credit to both their strong minds.

One great service to the suffrage cause Mrs. Bloomer did as early as 1850; it was she who made the introduction that initiated the firm and fruitful friendship between Elizabeth Cady Stanton and Susan B. Anthony.

In October, 1851, Mrs. Bloomer made a plain statement of her conversion to woman's suffrage, admitting her past mistakes with a candor for which there is little editorial precedent. Once more her common sense served her as wisdom.

We have abandoned the idea that forming societies and passing resolutions is going to close up the dens of vice and iniquity. We labored long in this field, and flattered ourself that good would come out of it, but we have grown wiser now, and can see that we were but battling the wind; so we have taken another course, . . . We unhesitatingly maintain that it is only through the ballot box that the iniquitous traffic can be reached; and until woman can carry her influence there, she need never hope to do aught in a public way towards subduing the foe.

Then came the bloomer.

The name of the benefactor who invented the Turkish costume remains for some future historian to discover. The locus of the invention was probably one of the "water cures," those hydropathic institutions to which the nineteenth-century lady retired for relief when her health and spirits gave way, as they often did, under the weight of household and maternal cares. The accounts of the hours that water cure patients spent packed in wet sheets are rather gruesome reading, though the treatment was probably relaxing, but the rest of the regimen had much in common with that of the modern sanitarium: a strict schedule carefully adhered to, wholesome diet, and prescribed exercise in the open air. But exercise, even walking, in the decades before the Civil War, was difficult for the female patient. Her dress was one of the most stupidly hampering and unhealthful ever imposed by fashion. Stays were laced so tight that both breath and motion were painful. Skirt and petticoats—a half-dozen was the correct number—hung from the hips. They weighed often as much as twelve pounds and were so long that they literally swept the ground, collecting dust and filth from floor or sidewalk. By changing this burden for Turkish trousers and a tunic the water cure patient could indulge in country walks and even perform calisthenics.

The Turkish dress as a working costume was tried by the women of the Oneida Community in the summer of 1848 when they undertook to do some vigorous carpentry, helping the men in the erection of a new communal dwelling, and they became so fond of their trousers that they refused to give them up when the work was finished. To wear the Turkish dress was established as part of the community practice.

These experiments were made behind walls. Mrs. Bloomer had never seen a Turkish costume when, in January, 1851, she read in the Seneca County *Courier* an editorial on "Female Attire." The writer, like many another contemporary editor, inveighed against the "inconvenience, unhealthfulness and discomfort" of woman's dress and then, surprising innovation, he went on to suggest a practical remedy: a change to "Turkish pantaloons and a skirt reaching a little below the knee."

Mrs. Bloomer clipped the paragraph with delight. Since her husband's growing law practice had caused him to sever his editorial connections, the *Courier* had been solidly opposing the *Lily* on the woman's rights question; now here was the "*Courier* man" seriously advising woman to "put on the pantaloons." This seemed to the *Lily*'s editor a very good joke. The *Courier*'s reply expressed surprise that the *Lily* should treat with levity so important a matter as the reform of female dress and Mrs. Bloomer fell immediately serious. She endorsed and approved the *Courier*'s recommendations.

And just at that moment the question ceased to be abstract: a pair of Turkish trousers walked down the tree-lined streets of Seneca Falls.

Elizabeth Smith Miller, after whom the bloomer should really have been named, was on a visit to her cousin Mrs. Stanton. Mrs. Miller was the first woman to wear the Turkish costume in public. She had put it on encouraged both by her husband and her father, that energetic reformer Gerrit Smith who believed that women would never accomplish anything really substantial for themselves or the world while they remained in their "clothes-prison" of petticoats and stays.

Mrs. Stanton, who was doing most of her housework and taking care of three small sons, looked at Cousin Libby with delighted admiration. Into a brief paragraph in her autobiography she has compressed all the daily weight of nineteenth-century woman's sartorial woe and all the exhilaration of her own release: "To see my cousin, with a lamp in one hand and a baby in the other, walk upstairs with ease and grace, while, with flowing robes, I pulled myself up with difficulty, lamp and baby out of the question, readily convinced me that there was sore need of reform in woman's dress, and I promptly donned a similar attire."

"She walked our streets," wrote Mrs. Bloomer, "in a skirt that came a little below the knees, and trousers of the same material—black satin. Having had part in the discussion of the dress question, it seemed proper that I should practice as I preached, and as the *Courier* man advised; and so a few days later I, too, donned the new costume, and in the next issue of my paper announced that fact to my readers." Before the year was out Amelia Bloomer was an international figure.

Horace Greeley's *Tribune* proclaimed her revolution and his exchanges all over the country picked up the article. The nation gaped in amusement and consternation. The whole strong-minded, woman's rights movement became suddenly a concrete issue. Mrs. Bloomer in her pantaloons was a symbol too plain to be ignored.

The name of the *Lily's* editor was immediately attached to the heterodox dress. It was called "the Bloomer costume"; "a Bloomer" was a woman who wore it. In vain the accurate and fair-minded editor explained that any credit for courage and inventiveness belonged not to her but to Elizabeth Smith Miller. Bloomer was a funnier word than Miller and the public declined to change. Mrs. Bloomer never used the word herself but "bloomer" has become part of the American language.

The country watched fascinated as the movement spread. The appearance of a Bloomer on the streets of any city was news. Their increase was reported as though they were some strange new fauna. One was observed in Syracuse, another in Oswego Landing, in Auburn, in Lawrence, Massachusetts, in Milwaukee. The *Lily* reprinted these accounts.

Oswego *Journal:*—Quite an excitement was produced at the steamboat landing day before yesterday, at the appearance of a couple of ladies with the short, Turkish dress. They were traveling in company with gentlemen, and were evidently people of cultivation.

Springfield *Republican:*—A lady in a short dress, and with loose trowsers, gathered at the ankle, passed through town a day or two since, and produced quite a sensation among those who chanced to be in and around the depot. Her dress was very rich, and we have the authority of a lady witness for saying that it was beautifully becoming.

Havana (N.Y.) *Journal:*—A number of the ladies of this village have already made their appearance (after night-fall) in the Turkish dress much to the surprise of some and the admiration of others.

The movement spread to the larger cities. Some of the more progressive magazines went so far as to publish bloomer fashion plates on the same page with "Just from Paris." When a Bloomer walked down Tremont Street in Boston *Gleason's Pictorial Drawing Room Companion* sent out a staff artist to make a drawing of her costume, complete to the last detail. Unfortunately that bloomer was a well-known courtesan, which set back the fashion in Boston, but in other parts of New England it flourished. The factory operatives of Lowell, those amazing young ladies whose high standard of culture European travelers were continually citing as an argument for American democracy, organized a Bloomer Institute. They met on Wednesday evenings for mutual improvement in literature, science, manners, and morals and "emancipation from the thraldom of that whimsical and dictatorial French goddess Fashion."

In the Middle West there were bloomer balls but "Of course the bloomer does not thrive in the South," the *Southern Literary Messenger* wrote severely. "Our ladies blush that their sisters anywhere descend to such things." Yet the fashion continued to spread. It even crossed the Atlantic to London, a more significant movement than Amelia Bloomer, who thought very little about the old world, realized. Englishwomen were not accustomed to accepting ideas from their American cousins but bloomerism interested so many of them that even such august publications as *Bentley's Miscellany* and *Chamber's Edinburgh Journal* discussed the movement seriously. Shortly after their London appearance bloomers were reported to have been seen in Ireland and in Spain and we know that they were lampooned in a Paris vaudeville skit, but the history of their continental ventures remains to be written.

The notoriety which the bloomer brought the *Lily* Mrs. Bloomer accepted with calm pleasure. Dress reform always seemed to her a comparatively minor matter but she was quick to see its propaganda value for the greater cause. She watched the *Lily's* subscription list climb into the thousands and noted happily that "the good woman's rights doctrines were thus scattered from Canada to Florida and from Maine to California." Competently she kept the issue alive in her columns, alternating theoretical comment with practical advice. For those who wanted to adopt it she described the dress in detail:

Our skirts have been robbed of about a foot of their former length, and a pair of loose trousers of the same material as the dress, substituted. These latter extend from the waist to the ankle, and may be gathered into a band and buttoned tight round the ankle, or, what we think decidedly prettier, gathered three or four times, half an inch apart, and drawn up to just sufficient width to permit the foot to pass through; they should be long enough to allow them to fall over the top of the gaiter and rest on the instep, and may be trimmed or not, to suit the taste of the wearer.

We make our *dress* the same as usual, except that we wear no bodice, or but a very slight one; the waist is loose and easy, and without whalebones, unless it be a very limber one in front and under each arm. It is better to dispense with them altogether. Our skirt is *full*, and falls a little below the knee. Some make the dress with a sack front, entire from the shoulder to the knee, a tight back, and skirt gathered in as usual to across the hips. The front confined by a belt, or cord and tassels. Others make them with a yoke at the neck, a full waist without a bodice, a belt set in, and full skirt. Each one must be guided by her own taste and judgment in the matter. Shawls must be abandoned, and a sack or mantilla take their place. A nice fitting boot or gaiter and a round hat, make the whole unique.

Finally Mrs. Bloomer introduced bloomer pictures. Both she and Mrs. Stanton had their daguerreotypes taken in the costume and engravings were made for the *Lily*. "We are not ambitious," wrote Mrs. Bloomer under her portrait in the issue of September, 1851, "to show our face to our readers; all we seek is to let them see just what an 'immodest' dress we are wearing, and about which people have made such an ado. We hope our lady readers will not be shocked at our 'masculine' appearance, or gentlemen mistake us for one of their own sex."

Newspaper comment on the dress, whether it emanated from New York or London, was rather heavily comic. It was always taken for granted that when women put on the trousers it was because they wanted to be men. Almost every Bloomer cartoon and joke is a variant on that theme, which must have been funnier in the 1850's than it is today. Young ladies in bloomers were shown usurping one or another masculine prerogative: smoking cigars, cracking whips, walking with bulldogs; while often, as a corollary, some male being is reduced to feminine simperings. Bloomers escorted young gentlemen home from church or the theater; they went down on their trousered knees to propose; they expected their husbands to cook the dinner or mind the baby. The stage took up the joke. In New York there were performances by Bloomer minstrels; Barnum's Museum put on a Bloomer Parade; audiences laughed at a farce called *The Bloomers, or Pets in Pants.* (A century later New York was laughing at a musical comedy called *Bloomer Girl* where the trousers once so comically revolutionary were displayed as comically quaint.)

Mrs. Bloomer bore up serenely under the laughter and the jeers. A correspondent of the Boston *Museum*, who had evidently watched her closely on her lecture tours through New York State, writes that when boys taunt her on the street she shows neither mortification nor anger but is "both *blind* and *deaf* to everything that passes; and her countenance continues to express that same purity and happiness within, that would be expected from a child of fifteen, engaged in cultivating a bed of flowers." Mrs. Bloomer did have the heartening advantage of looking well in the costume. She was a piquant little figure in her trousers, not a funny one like some of her fellow suffragists.

To printed ridicule she was also happily blind but against the serious opponents of dress reform she went stoutly to battle. The most dangerous attacks she had to meet were theological. The awful divines, accustomed to silencing women with texts from St. Paul, now withdrew to Deuteronomy 22:5: "The woman shall not wear that which pertaineth unto a man." Mrs. Bloomer, who

A Bloomer cartoon from *Harper's Monthly Magazine*, August,
1851

had long since thought her way out of the theological thicket around woman's sphere, countered with Genesis.

There are laws of fashion in dress [she wrote in a long review of an anti-bloomer sermon] older than Moses, and it would be as sensible for the preacher to direct us to them as to him. The first fashion we have any record of was set us by Adam and Eve, and we are not told that there was any difference in the styles worn by them. "And they sewed fig leaves together, and made themselves aprons:" Genesis, iii, 7. Nothing here to show that his apron was bifurcated, and hers not, that hers was long and his short. We are led to suppose that they were just alike.

Some of the *Lily's* subscribers also had moral scruples about wearing the bloomer but they were of a different color. A group of "old ladies" wrote to inquire whether it would harm the cause if women of fifty or sixty adopted the costume. Mrs. Bloomer's reply was characteristic.

Do just as your impulses move you to do.—What you find a burthen in belief or apparel cast off. Woman has always sacrificed her comfort to fashion. You old women of sixty have been slaves to the tyrant long enough, and as you have but a few years to live, be as free and as happy as you can what time remains. Fit yourselves for a higher sphere, and cease grovelling in the dirt. Let there be no stain of earth upon your soul or apparel.

When bloomerism had been raging for a year and Mrs. Bloomer was firmly entrenched in the public mind as a symbol of strong-mindedness, she took a still deeper step into opprobrium: she appeared on a lecture platform. In the spring of 1852 Rochester had a two-day temperance meeting attended by some two thousand people. Mrs.

Bloomer was asked to address the delegates and chose to discuss woman's right to divorce a drunken husband, a dangerous subject, entangling temperance with the woman question, but she carried it off well. She has left us unfortunately no record of her oratorical emotions—perhaps she had none—nor any account of the logic by which she freed herself from the bonds of St. Paul. She seems to have stepped onto the platform as smoothly and competently as she sat down in the editorial chair. From the day of the Rochester speech both the temperance and the woman's rights movements reckoned her among their lecture assets. Her addresses were admired for their originality of approach as well as for sound reasoning and affecting exhortation. She spoke with warmth and conviction but was never emotional enough for spontaneous oratory; she always carefully wrote her speeches out beforehand.

Not long after the meeting in Rochester Mrs. Bloomer addressed the Temperance Convention in Albany and was one of a committee of three who carried into the astonished presence of the State Legislature a basket containing a monster prohibition petition signed by thirty thousand women. A publicity stunt of that kind was an innovation and the attention it attracted was great. She next made a successful tour through the state and was then invited to speak in New York City with Miss Anthony, Mrs. L. N. Fowler, and the Reverend Antoinette Brown. The audiences at each of their three meetings were reported to be as large and respectable as those that gathered to hear Jenny Lind.

Mrs. Bloomer's experience with the costume was seldom irksome but Mrs. Stanton, Miss Anthony, and the other suffragists who had put on the pantaloons began after a few years to feel them more of a burden than the long skirts had been. The rowdy songs and hootings which greeted them on the streets of any strange city became unbearably tiresome; the public seemed never to grasp the lesson they were trying to teach; and they felt that curiosity about their dress distracted the attention of audiences from the fundamental doctrines they were chiefly concerned to preach. By 1853 Mrs. Stanton was writing to Miss Anthony: "I hope, Susan, you have let down a dress and petticoat. The cup of ridicule is greater than you can bear. It is not wise, Susan, to use up so much energy and feeling in that way. You can put them to better use. I speak from experience."

Most of the suffragists gave up the costume at about that time but Mrs. Miller continued to wear it for three years more and Mrs. Bloomer did not put it off till 1859.

While the Turkish costume was doing its work of reform the Bloomers became practical as well as spiritual pioneers. Dexter Bloomer had as strongly as his wife the impulse to shape a better world and Seneca Falls was already set in its form. He wanted to build something new, to have a share in the moulding of the young continent. In the fall of 1853 the couple set out on an exploratory trip to the Middle West, Dexter scouting for business opportunities while Amelia spoke on temperance and woman's enfranchisement in such flourishing cities as Cleveland, Indianapolis, Detroit, Chicago, and Milwaukee. It was real missionary work that she did; except for a visit in the 'forties from the intrepid Lucy Stone, not one of those progressive metropolises had ever seen a woman on a public platform. Curiosity brought out large audiences. "The Bloomer" had no illusions about their motives but she managed to find a silver lining in most hard facts. "If the dress drew the crowds that came to hear me," she wrote, "it was well. They heard the message I brought them, and it has borne abundant fruit."

Dexter Bloomer's investigations resulted in the purchase of an interest in the *Western Home Visitor*, published in Mount Vernon, Ohio, and dedicated to "all reformatory questions designed to advance the interests of the community." In February, 1854, the couple moved their possessions west.

Seneca Falls was genuinely sorry to lose them. No less than five hundred members of the little community gathered at a banquet, organized by the Good Templars, to bid them Godspeed with appropriate speeches and resolutions.

The *Lily* went west with its editor and flourished in Ohio soil. The circulation, now national in extent, rose from four thousand to six. Mrs. Bloomer served also as assistant editor of the *Home Visitor*, writing an article for it every week.

Two small but significant battles she waged and won in Mount Vernon. Invited to lecture in Ohio and Indiana, she one night spoke from a platform recently occupied by Horace Mann. The house she drew was quite as large as his so she asked for as large a fee. The lecture committee were astonished at the suggestion that a woman's worth should be reckoned by her accomplishment, but they gave her the money.

A little later Mrs. Bloomer threw the printing office into consternation by introducing a woman typesetter for the

Lily. The outraged masculine printers went on strike. When logic, reason, and moral suasion failed, the Bloomers with imperturbable common sense dismissed all their printers and organized a new staff with four women typesetters and three enlightened males for the heavier tasks. The revolutionary arrangement worked; the two papers appeared with exemplary regularity.

The Bloomers seem to have liked Mount Vernon but they stayed only a year. Their eyes looked further west; they wanted a newer country with more scope. It is quite probable, too, that they were alarmed by the terrible epidemic of cholera which swept through Ohio in the spring of 1854. Coupled with a severe drought up and down the Ohio valley, it turned the thoughts of many denizens of the state towards Iowa, reported by the medical journals to be the second healthiest section of the nation and by its guidebooks to have a rich black soil very easy to work. The state had been admitted to the Union in 1846, peacefully, as anti-slavery territory. Its Indians were quiet. Its treeless prairies could be put under cultivation without the usual heartbreaking labor of clearing the land. Iowa, in short, offered all the delights of pioneering without the usual perils.

In July Dexter Bloomer made a prospecting trip west and found himself so nearly in agreement with the emigrants' guides that he bought a house in Iowa's western-most city, Council Bluffs, and in the spring the Bloomers became pioneers.

Conestoga wagons poured into Iowa at the rate of a thousand a day during 1855 but the Bloomers, being city dwellers not farmers, made the journey by boat, up the Missouri from St. Louis to St. Joseph. There, since the river was too low for further travel, they took stage for a hard two-day trip across the prairie.

Only a few hours before the coach was scheduled to start, the citizens of St. Joseph discovered that they had a distinguished lady in their midst and the national passion for lectures, nowhere stronger than in the West, asserted itself. A committee of gentlemen waited upon Mrs. Bloomer and begged an address on woman's rights. It was seven o'clock; the coach left at ten; they said they would have an audience for her by eight. And, to her amazement, they did; a tall Negro went about the streets with a bell shouting the good news of her appearance at the courthouse.

Whenever Mrs. Bloomer writes of Iowa she sounds a lyric note. The booster and the reformer are near kin. A city new built, without a past, may well be a good and golden city. To raise in the wilderness a town like Council Bluffs is one more way of bringing in the millennium.

The euphonious name, Iowa [her chapter in the *History of Woman Suffrage* begins], signifying "the beautiful land," is peculiarly appropriate to those gently undulating prairies, decorated in the season of flowers with a brilliant garniture of honey-suckles, jassamines, wild-roses and violets, watered with a chain of picturesque lakes and rivers, chasing each other into the bosom of the boundless Mississippi. The motto on the great seal of the State, "Our liberties we prize and our rights we will maintain," is the key-note to the successive struggles made there to build up a community of moral, virtuous, intelligent people, securing justice, liberty and equality to all.

The stagecoach that took the Bloomers across the undulating prairies set them down, decidedly weary, before

Council Bluffs' most imposing edifice, the three-story brick Pacific Hotel erected to catch the emigrant trade. The fixed population of the city was something less than three thousand but Council Bluffs already saw itself as the great railway center it was to become. Frame houses were building among the dwellings of hewn logs and the streets had names even when they were only beaten tracks through sunflower fields. There was a Methodist Church and the Congregationalists were putting up a new brick structure though the minister preached at present from a drygoods box in an unplastered frame building; a United States land office was going up; daily stages ran south and east; and land a few miles outside the city was selling at $10 an acre.

The Bloomers' house was on Bancroft Street, now Fourth, not far from Willow Avenue, with an unobstructed view of the "mighty Missouri" three miles below. Indians camped in Turley's Glen near by and the number of saloons within earshot must have been a little discouraging to the editor of the *Lily* but Amelia set enthusiastically to work to make a home. She had not much to do it with for not until July did the river rise enough to float the freight boat with their household goods. The uncarpeted floors of her two rooms were a trial to the good nineteenth-century housekeeper but she managed to borrow a table, two old wooden chairs, a stove, a few dishes, and a mattress which they laid on the floor. They had also three trunks which, Mrs. Bloomer related with amused composure, she used for seats when receiving her first callers.

Social life began at once and it was, in many ways, Dexter Bloomer recorded, an ideal state of society: "everybody knew everybody else, and all whose characters were clear and untarnished met each other on a footing of perfect equality." Against the strong fresh winds that blew across the prairies the formalities and conventions of the East could not stand; but Council Bluffs, though it thought itself in advance of Mount Vernon and Seneca Falls, was consciously building to the same ideal pattern. Churches, newspapers, schools were reckoned with pride as their number increased. The formation of a literary club, a library association, a lyceum were matters for congratulation. Culture was as important to the community as the price of land.

The blossoming metropolis saw at once that the Bloomers were highly desirable citizens. The community incorporated them almost before they had shaken the dust from their traveling clothes. Not three days after her arrival Amelia was invited to the annual meeting of the Congregational Ladies Sewing Circle and found herself, despite her Episcopalian affiliations, elected to its presidency and scheming a fair to raise money for the flooring of the new church. Other duties and dignities followed fast.

Dexter Bloomer found his place as swiftly and as neatly. He is a conspicuous example of that quality of enlightened self-interest which so fascinated de Tocqueville in the American character. His humanitarianism, his patriotism, and his business acumen interlocked. He established a lucrative law practice in Council Bluffs because he was as honest as St. Ives and as benevolent. The firm of Bloomer and Kinsman became known as agents for five eastern insurance companies. They gave "particular attention to the Collection of Debts." They made themselves experts on land claims, selecting and entering land in both Iowa and Nebraska, purchasing warrants and city property, buying and selling farms and wild lands. In 1861 Dexter Bloomer was named Receiver for the United States Land Office. And all the while he invested for himself in land and railroad stock as carefully and honestly as he did for his clients. He was soon a very solid citizen.

When the Civil War began he opened a recruiting station in his office and agreed to serve as chairman of the Committee in Charge of Donations to Soldiers' Families. He worked for the Christian Commission and the Sanitary Commission. Nearly a hundred soldiers' families were grateful to his efficient administration for their stove wood and groceries during the hard war winters. Soldiers in the field got in the habit of sending Dexter Bloomer the portions of their pay they wanted turned over to their relatives. In a single month in 1865 he administered $1,700 for the men of the Twenty-Ninth Iowa. When peace had been declared and the men were coming home he advertised that he was prepared to collect promptly "all arrearages of bounty, pay or pension," and the veterans were only too glad to enlist his services. When he was elected mayor of Council Bluffs in 1869 even the opposition newspapers referred to him as a "straight forward, honest man." It was not long before a substantial business block bore the Bloomer name, and that name was later attached to a grade school, christened in recognition of Dexter Bloomer's long presidency of the School Board. "The father of the public-school system of the city" he was called when, in 1890, the Bloomers' golden wedding anniversary took on something of the character of a civic celebration.

That anniversary party paid homage to Mrs. Bloomer

also as a leading citizen though she had supposed when she set out for Iowa that she was retiring into private life. She had sold her *Lily*, for it was quite obvious that even the most indulgent of subscribers would become impatient with the irregular appearances of a magazine printed three hundred miles from a railroad. The purchaser was a Mrs. Mary Birdsall who conducted the Ladies Department of the *Indiana Farmer*. She ran the *Lily* competently enough —Mrs. Bloomer contributed frequently—but its personality was gone and after a few years it died unnoticed.

Her editorial garments Mrs. Bloomer put off without expressed regret. She had liked getting out the *Lily* but she also liked to cook, to tend the big beds of asters on her new lawn, and to make the currant jelly that took prizes at the Pottawattamie County fairs; she liked, in fact, almost any work her hand found to do. Duty done was for her synonymous with happiness, a conjunction which sounds strangely in twentieth-century ears. Her temperance and woman's rights propaganda she had never thought of as a career and for personal fame she did not care at all; the important thing was to hasten the millennium. Making a home in a new territory was a definite contribution to that end. So was the raising of a family. The Bloomers, who had always wanted children, adopted, soon after they settled in Council Bluffs, a brother and sister whom they educated and cared for till they were ready to start pioneer homes of their own.

It was this role of pioneer wife and mother which, oddly enough, caused Mrs. Bloomer to abandon her pioneer dress. Making new friends and going to her first parties in Council Bluffs she found it pleasanter to be an individual rather than a symbol of reform; she "felt at times like donning long skirts," and did so. The winds of Iowa, moreover, were strong; sweeping across leagues of open prairie, gathering enormous force, they "played sad havoc with short skirts when I went out, and I was greatly annoyed and mortified by having my skirts turned over my head and shoulders on the street." Yet she liked the Turkish dress so much for housework and believed so thoroughly in the liberty it represented that she persisted in wearing it until the Empress Eugénie invented the hoop skirt. Hoops, Amelia Bloomer found, were light and pleasant to wear; they did away with the necessity for heavy underskirts which had been her great objection to the old street-sweeping costume. To keep up two wardrobes, a long and a short, was both inconvenient and expensive so she discarded the bloomer costume. "I consulted my own feelings and inclination and judgment in laying it off," she wrote, "never dreaming but I had the same right to doff that I had to don it."

The citizens of Iowa were glad to find The Bloomer so good a home body but they had no intention of letting her public talents rust. She had not, as she discovered at St. Joseph, crossed the Mississippi incognita. Six months after her arrival in Council Bluffs she was lecturing on temperance from the pulpit of the Congregational Church; then in the Methodist Church on "Woman's Enfranchisement," with such effect that she was asked to cross the river and repeat her address before the Nebraska State Legislature. A crowded council chamber received her with cheers and the Omaha correspondent of the Council Bluffs *Chronotype* set down the most detailed description we have of her platform manner:

We watched her closely, and saw that she was perfectly self-possessed—not a nerve seemed to be moved by excitement, and the voice did not tremble. She arose in the dignity of a true woman, as if the importance of her mission so absorbed her thoughts that timidity or bashfulness were too mean to entangle the mental powers. She delivered her lecture in a pleasing, able, and I may say eloquent manner that enchained the attention of her audience for an hour and a half. A *man* could not have beaten it. . . . Mrs. Bloomer, though a little body, is among the great women of the United States.

A bill to confer the suffrage on women was passed by the House but a filibuster on another measure prevented its being acted upon in the upper chamber before the close of the session and by the next session the temper of the legislature had changed.

Her eloquence in Omaha spread Mrs. Bloomer's fame as a lecturer and thereafter she was in constant demand, for no Western town which wanted to be thought progressive could afford to be without its lecture course. Women's rights and women's education were her chief topics but she talked also on temperance and organized through the state lodges of the Good Templars which she had joined in Seneca Falls. She wrote frequently for papers in Iowa and in Chicago and kept up a vigorous Iowa propaganda among her Eastern friends, describing the satisfactions of pioneering and urging women as well as men to take up land. "I do wish," runs a letter written in 1855, "that more women would become owners of the soil, and I am especially anxious that you, Mrs. Vaughan, and those women who labored so untiringly with you in the cause of humanity, should come in for a share."

Iowa came to take it for granted that when the feminine point of view needed expression Mrs. Bloomer's was the voice through which it should speak. It was she who, in

1861, presented to Company B of the Fourth Iowa the large silk flag stitched for them by the patriotic ladies of Council Bluffs. (It was made in the Bloomer parlor together with 122 havelocks, 174 towels, 12 needlebooks, 20 bed sacks, 50 pillow sacks, and 14 cotton and feather pillows.) As Company B listened to Mrs. Bloomer's address "many a brawny breast heaved," the local press reported, "and tears trickled down many a manly face."

It was Mrs. Bloomer who, in the summer of 1865, traveled to Chicago to attend the great Northwest Sanitary Fair and to report that Iowa's booth made a "very creditable appearance in fancy articles and curiosities."

It was Mrs. Bloomer, in 1870, who took the lead in the organization of the Iowa State Suffrage Society, became its second president, and worked actively in that office for many years.

To Mrs. Bloomer was given credit for the clauses in the Revised Code of Iowa (1873) which abolished the legal distinction between men and women in the matter of holding property.

And Mrs. Bloomer, though now so thoroughly identified with Iowa, was by no means forgotten in the East. In 1867 the American Equal Suffrage Association made her a vice president, an office which she held till the end of her life (she died in 1894), and summoned her frequently to Washington and New York for support and counsel.

As the reporter of the *Chronotype* had seen, Amelia Bloomer, though a little body, is among the great citizens of the United States. Not many of her contemporaries did so much for "the emancipation of women from intemperance, injustice, prejudice and bigotry."

"Grace Greenwood"

Sara J. C. Lippincott, as engraved for *Godey's Lady's Book*, December, 1848, and photographed for *Victoria Magazine*, London, August 1870

Greenwood Leaves

"GRACE GREENWOOD"
(SARA J. C. LIPPINCOTT)

T HE white horse broke into a merry gallop, his hooves
barely dinting the hard wet sand. The rider's dark
eyes glistened; she leaned back in her saddle, graceful and
at ease. Her long skirt was wet with the wind-blown
spray; so was the wide-brimmed hat and the plume that
drooped picturesquely against her shoulder, but she was
not dismayed. "Undine," she thought, "sunrise on the
sea; an hour to be savored with full heart and fixed forever in a song."

"Grace Greenwood" had written a good many descriptions in that kind for *Graham's Magazine* and Mr. Godey's
Lady's Book but she did not usually apply them to herself. At this high moment, though, this late summer day in
1853, she felt it legitimate to pose as one of her own heroines, for to the literary "fame" which she had been enjoying for half a dozen years was now added love. Leander,
tall, handsome, and accomplished, had offered her his hand.
It was a climactic moment, one of those in which one
feels compelled to review the past. Reining her horse to
a walk she devoted herself to that absorbing occupation,
finding it agreeable even though her romantic mood was

punctured now and then by a shaft from her straight thinking, observant mind.

It had been a happy life, its lines falling for the most part in pleasant places. "Grace Greenwood's" reputation as a "new woman" had frightened away some timid suitors but Leander loved her the better for having a head as well as a heart and she had long ago convinced herself that the literary and the domestic virtues could be cultivated side by side.

For her ability as a poet "Grace Greenwood" thanked her mother—except in the matter of her name. Could there be a more uncompromisingly unliterary appellation than Sara Jane Clarke (even though Sara, as she liked to note, means Princess)? The Clarkes were good Puritan stock, kin to the great Jonathan Edwards, and Sara's father, Dr. Thaddeus, had been a physician of repute in Lebanon, Connecticut, before ill-health caused his retirement. The family were living near Syracuse, New York, in Pompey, that loveliest of villages set upon a hill, when Sara was born, on September 23, 1823, the youngest daughter among eleven children.

She was, so they told her, "a little dark-eyed gypsy of a child," much less interested in the conventional games of small girls than in playing with dogs and ponies and tagging about after big brothers and cousins while they fished and hunted. By contemporary standards Sara ran wild and she saw enough of other children to appreciate her freedom. Freedom, in fact, by the time she was in her teens, became for her a definite and important concept; throughout her life she never wrote the word without emotion. Her youthful notions concerning freedom were romantic but not altogether inaccurate. She read Byron and bled for Greece; listened to the table talk of an intelligent household and grew indignant for the oppressed Italians, Irish, and Magyars; learned to think of Negro slavery as a dark blot on the American scutcheon. She felt, too, an imaginative sympathy for anyone deprived of sunlight and fresh air which developed, as she grew older, into a humanitarian concern with prison reform.

Sara's mind was as quick and active as her body. She liked going to school in the growing towns of Fabius and Rochester to which the family subsequently moved—western New York was pioneer country in those days—and she liked reading with her mother, always her special instructor and guide. Of New England Huguenot and Puritan stock, Deborah Baker Clarke was blessed with a sound education, including a familiarity with the English classics greater than that of most housewives of her generation, and, so her friends recorded, with both "breadth and delicacy of mind."

The Clarkes were a talkative family. Sara was encouraged to say what she thought and soon took to writing down her thoughts as well. She was gifted with that fluency which the nineteenth century so often mistook for inspiration and by the time she was nineteen—the family were settled then in New Brighton, Pennsylvania —she was seeing her work in print. She published at first in the anti-slavery journals, "mostly poems (so-called), pouring out my hot heart in protests, rebukes and Cassandra-like prophecies." These "crude, but passionately earnest" productions did, she felt when she reread them at seventy, train her in "fearless and natural expression." They made lasting friends for her, too, among the abolitionists, but they brought in no money and Sara was beginning to feel that she should be responsible for her own support. She tried her hand at writing for the literary magazines which paid for contributions, and met with immediate success. In 1844 N. P. Willis, then editing the *New Mirror*, printed this note in his weekly "Breviary" of verse:

Another of the gifted *unheard-ofs* is Miss Sarah [sic] J. Clarke, a very youthful poetess, who has the rare gift of patience in polishing her verse. Mrs. Hemans would have placed a very even feather in her wing of majestic soarings had she written what has been sent us for the New Mirror by this girl of seventeen—the following invocation "To Mother Earth:"

Seventeen was a characteristic Willis gallantry; Miss Clarke was twenty-one and her friends were beginning to wonder whether she would ever marry. She was handsome, though tall for contemporary taste, but rather overpoweringly exuberant and clever. She was already spoken of as a bluestocking and even as that much worse, because more belligerent, creature, a new woman.

The ease with which a very average maker of verses could command a public in the days before the Civil War, the speed with which anyone a little above the average became a "genius," is indicative of the young republic's eagerness for a national literature. It is remarkable that the fluttering flock of female poets kept their heads at all under the glittering adjectives showered upon them weekly by the reviews. Listen, for instance, to Anne Lynch, writing in *Godey's Lady's Book* on Sara Clarke:

We call these poems Sapphic, and the fragments of Sappho which have come down to us do not surpass them; but they compare more nearly with some of those impassioned strains that have burst from the heart of Mrs. Norton.

And Sara Clarke, in the *Saturday Evening Post*, on Miss Lynch:

The strength and freedom, and high moral purity of her genius, fill me with reverential admiration. She delivers the divine oracles, solemn truths and sublime prophecies, not in the harsh tones of malediction and rebuke, but through the subduing sweetness of song, the winning melody of verse.

The Sapphic poet was skillful also at prose numbers. She began for Willis' *Mirror* and *Home Journal* a series of lively informal Letters which caught the public fancy. To sign them she invented the pseudonym "Grace Greenwood," and the simple symbolism appeared to her friends and acquaintances so appropriate that before long they were all addressing her as Grace.

That the impassioned poems and the saucy Letters flowed from the same pen seemed to Grace Greenwood's contemporaries deliciously piquant. They found her enthusiasm and her lively curiosity refreshing; they enjoyed her wit; and they considered "artlessness" a literary virtue. In addition they credited her with originality for, though she never overstepped the bounds of female delicacy, her interests ranged beyond the usual limits of woman's sphere and her vocabulary was more virile and pungent than that of most of her sisters. Willis thought this "a peculiarity which she had better cultivate than abate."

Part of the originality of the Letters derived from their writer's Puritan heritage which constrained her to speak out boldly those things that she believed: that, for instance, aggressive war is wicked; that capital punishment is wrong; that Ireland is oppressed (her friend Anne Lynch was the daughter of an Irish exile); that Mrs. Fanny Kemble Butler has a right to wear trousers on her country walks. "To my ambushed correspondents," wrote Grace Greenwood in a Letter to the *Post,* "who have chosen to remonstrate with me for my opinions upon certain moral subjects, putting their politic advisings against my honest convictions, I would respectfully say that while my soul is my own, it shall speak its own language, in the freedom which is its priceless and inalienable birthright."

The Letters, except for their prolixity and their gush of language, are near kin to such modern newspaper columns as "My Day." Cities and scenery visited, books read, paintings and statues gazed upon, interesting people met and talked with, are all recorded in a blithe certainty that the reader will be as wholeheartedly interested as the writer. And apparently he was. Soon Grace Greenwood was writing for *Godey's, Graham's, Sartain's,* and the *Saturday Evening Post* as well as the *Home Journal.* She was editor for a time of Godey's *Lady's Dollar Newspaper* and editorial associate of his *Lady's Book* with its nearly 150,000 subscribers. "I had no power except to offer mild suggestions and appeals for mercy toward young aspirants, to the senior editor [Sarah Josepha Hale]—an experienced and hardened old lady—who seemed to me to sit all day in and on piles of manuscript and to sleep in proof-sheets."

Godey himself Grace Greenwood found genial and not illiberal as a paymaster but unfortunately for their connection one of the subjects on which her soul insisted on speaking out was the freedom of the slave. When her friend John Greenleaf Whittier asked her to write something for the *National Era*, of which he was contributing editor, she readily complied. Presently the appearance of her name in the *Era's* columns was noted in the South and in December, 1849, the Columbia, South Carolina, *Telegraph* printed an angry denunciation of the *Lady's Book* because its junior editor was contributing to an abolition journal. This, they suggested, was "an argument against lining Northern pockets with Southern cash."

Trembling for his Southern lining Louis Godey sent the *Telegraph* an abject letter accompanied by the January issue of his magazine with Grace Greenwood's name withdrawn from the cover, "where it was placed nominally as editor, she never having had the least control over its columns." In the February number the name was restored. Whether this was an attempt on Godey's part to have his cake as well as eat it or whether, as Grace herself charitably believed, it was a printer's error, she felt it imperative to publish in the newspapers a spirited "card" in which she begged leave to state to her friends that the restoration had been made without her knowledge and that she had no longer any connection of any kind with the *Lady's Book*. The incident attracted editorial comment both North and South and Whittier sprang to her defense. In "Lines on a Portrait" (which had just been published in the *Lady's Book*) he described the publisher's "moony breadth of virgin face, by thought unviolated."

The editor of the *Era* gallantly offered Miss Greenwood a position to replace the one she had lost by writing for him and invited her to stay with his family in Washington. The *Saturday Evening Post* commissioned her as

Washington correspondent and in June, 1850, she made her first visit to the capital.

Dr. Gamaliel Bailey, editor of the *Era*, is one of the most engaging figures among the abolitionists. Though trained as a physician and with a record of heroic service during the cholera epidemic of 1832, he decided to devote himself to journalism and, when he had been converted by Theodore Weld from colonization to abolition, joined James Birney in the editorship of the *Philanthropist*, the first anti-slavery paper in the West. Three times their Cincinnati printing office was sacked, press and type thrown into the Ohio, and the editors threatened with death. Bailey was well schooled therefore in his profession when he undertook the editorship of the *National Era* which, convinced that the cause needed a journal speaking from the capital, Lewis Tappan had established in Washington in 1847. A year later Bailey was facing a mob which besieged his house in E Street.

Grace Greenwood told the story in an article written for the *Cosmopolitan* (February, 1890) when she was nearly seventy.

Dr. Bailey displayed not alone Napoleonic courage, but that rarer Napoleonic charm or magnetism which moves and sub-jugates masses of men. He and his wife were alone in the house, having sent their children and servants to a place of safety. Hearing his name called by a hundred peremptory voices, he walked out on the steps, and stood there in the light of the hall lamp, a fair mark for a hundred pistol-shots, as he quietly said: "*I* am Dr. Bailey. What is your wish?" When, after much confused shouting, they made their modest de-mand for the immediate surrender of his property and his rights, on pain of receiving a coat of tar and feathers, he respectfully declined to give or take, but asked to be heard in his own defense, and, for a wonder, they consented. He spoke to them in the frank, fearless, "let-us-reason-together" style peculiar to him. Yet Paul preaching at Athens scarce displayed more courage and dignity, or more splendid tact. The result was marvelous. Every instant he gained on their prejudices; threats of lynching ceased, and murmurs of assent and approval were heard here and there in the surging crowd. Men who came to curse remained to cheer—not only the plucky abolition editor, but the brave wife, who now stood at his side. Strangest of all, a well-known Washington man, whose devotion to Southern institutions could not be doubted, and who was with the mob, if not of it, leaped upon the steps and made an earnest speech against haste and violence, and in favor of the right of a man to his own property—of an American citizen to free speech and a free press. So effective were both appeals, that when the last speaker moved an adjournment, the crowd, with but one dissenting voice, voted for it and quietly dispersed—some actually calling back, "Good-night, doctor!" And that was the end of it.

From this time, *The National Era*, guided by a wise head and a firm will, pursued a prosperous career and became a power, not alone as the organ of the Free Soil party, but for its moral dignity and unusual literary excellence.

To the young Grace Greenwood association with the *Era* was cause for literary pride. Not only Whittier, whom she thought "brimful of genius," wrote for its pages but also Theodore Parker, Henry B. Stanton, Bayard Taylor, the poet sisters Alice and Phoebe Carey, "Gail Hamilton," Mrs. Southworth; and, in 1852, the young editor's duties included the reading of proof on "Uncle Tom's Cabin."

Eighteen fifty was the summer of "the memorable 'Long

Session' which witnessed the momentous struggle on the Compromise measures and the passage of the Fugitive Slave Law." The Bailey household went daily to the Senate gallery. It was a gay social season, too, with receptions, banquets, concerts, and plays, and Miss Greenwood had letters of introduction which took her into circles more elegant than the Baileys'. Henry Clay himself tried to convert her from abolitionism, but "I could see," she wrote, "that my abolition sentiments and associations were regarded with suspicion or lofty disapprobation; so, naturally, I affiliated more and more with the ostracized party." (The "naturally" in that sentence is characteristic.) "I liked that little militant band of Free-Soilers— men of sharply defined characters, having the courage of their opinions. I liked their wives and daughters—for the most part bright, intelligent, earnest women. We knew we had been 'sent to Coventry,' and set about making 'Coventry' a jolly sort of place."

In 1851 the Baileys moved to a spacious house on C Street and their informal Saturday evenings became an institution; "An American Salon" Grace Greenwood called her reminiscent article. Dress and refreshments were of the simplest—"What! no brandy and water?" growled Thackeray when he was handed coffee; there was no music, no dramatic reading, but men and women who enjoyed good talk liked to come and the gathering took on "much of the character of the old French *salon*, except that it was more cosmopolitan, and had a purer moral atmosphere." Even Southerners "fearless or curious enough" were welcome; men like Charles Sumner and Thaddeus Stevens were in the habit of dropping in; philanthropists came and reformers, gentlemen of the press, and distinguished foreigners. Grace Greenwood tells with amusement of her futile attempt, one Saturday evening, to reconvert to abolitionism Fredrika Bremer "won over from the pure faith" by her lionization in the South. Mrs. Bailey was Grace's idea of the perfect hostess and the perfect wife: her life, "though loyally merged, was not hidden in that of her husband."

Grace Greenwood believed that she was the first female Washington correspondent. She seems to have been unaware of the fiery sortie of Mrs. Swisshelm in the *Tribune*, which had culminated just before her arrival, but she was, in any case, a daring pioneer and she held the field for an unprecedentedly long period, writing Washington Letters at intervals from 1850 until 1897. The early Letters are rather more occupied with the personalities of the nation's legislators than with their policies but the writer made her own political sympathies so clear that the *Post* felt constrained to run an editorial note to put on record, "what all sensible people will know, without our stating it, *that we do not hold ourselves responsible in the least, for Grace's opinions of men and things*."

In the same year in which she began her Washington Letters Grace Greenwood published her first book, a collection of Letters and sketches which Ticknor and Fields had proposed as early as 1847, inaugurating with that suggestion a warm publisher-author friendship. "Artless" as Grace was in her writing she was a shrewd businesswoman. It was she who suggested delaying the appearance of her volume until her appointment as junior editor of the *Lady's Book* had been announced, though she had already, as she wrote Fields, a good measure of fame: a Mississippi steamboat had been christened *Grace*

Greenwood, and so had a Kentucky racehorse (though he ran only a poor second). It was Grace who invented the title *Greenwood Leaves;* she who declined to make a second collection (1852) until it was quite certain that no more editions of the first could be sold; she who urged the firm to greater effort in supplying copies to bookshops in the West where her friends often found them difficult to obtain. She collected for Ticknor and Fields also in 1850 some stories for children which she called *The History of My Pets* and, a year later, her *Poems*. When, in 1852, she planned a tour in Europe she arranged that they should bring out in book form the Letters she purposed writing for the *Era*. Dr. Bailey who had been paying her $500 a year for her Letters and editorial services, was glad to have her as foreign correspondent but when she wrote from London asking him to increase the stipend to a thousand so that she might continue her travels to Rome, he declined, and in April Grace, somewhat ungratefully, transferred her correspondence to the more affluent *Saturday Evening Post*.

"Greenwood Leaves from Over the Sea" bubble with excitement and enthusiasm, detailing in tireless superlatives encounters with the antique shrines and contemporary celebrities of England, France, Germany, and Italy. As *Haps and Mishaps of a Tour in Europe* they made the most popular book that Grace Greenwood ever published; it was still being reprinted in the 'nineties. The modern reader, who travels to collect not emotions but facts, is likely to share the sentiments of the London *Athenæum* (November 18, 1854): "'Sunny Memories' appear to be setting in with great severity. We had hoped that Mrs. Stowe had flung enough of rosy hues and golden tints about this honest, unpretending, murky London . . . to satisfy America for one generation at least." They quote at length an account of a dinner at Charles Dickens' to warn their readers at what a price they receive into their homes the "wandering sisterhood of the quill from America."

The parts of the book most agreeable today to English or American readers are not the noble sentiments inspired by the Venus de Milo, Miss Mitford, or the Matterhorn but the strong-minded bits of straight reporting. The whole trip, as a matter of fact, was strong-minded. To go abroad alone in the 1850's was pioneering for an "unprotected female" even though she carefully attached herself at each stage of her journey to parties of friends. Miss Clarke, moreover, frequently left the beaten track. Her British visit included not only the conventional excursion to Scotland in homage to Burns and Waverly but three weeks in Ireland where delight in scenery and Celtic ruins was mingled with observation of the condition of the oppressed peasantry. Everywhere she visited prisons, almshouses, and hospitals for the insane.

It may be thought strange [she writes] that I should go to these hospitals alone; but I had in Venice no friends whose sightseeing tastes lay in that direction, and I believed that I ought to visit and report upon some institutions of the kind in Italy. Moreover, I must confess that madness has ever had a terrible fascination for me, and that, at times, I like to test my own strength to look down into the profoundest depths of human suffering.

There were even more interesting incidents in the trip on which she was discreetly silent. It was with Charlotte

Cushman, for instance, that she lived in Rome; Harriet Hosmer, the sculptress, was of the party; and Grace Greenwood herself was watched during her stay by the Italian police because she was known to be a friend of Mazzini.

Other reasons besides the desire for travel had prompted the European journey. The asthma from which Miss Clarke had long suffered had grown worse and she was advised to try the Italian climate. There was a romantic reason also: Grace Greenwood had been crossed in love.

In the Baileys' hospitable parlors she had met a handsome, witty Philadelphian, Leander K. Lippincott. He was generally considered a young man of parts and promise though he was at the time devoting the major portion of his energies to the fluttering of feminine hearts. Grace fell promptly under his spell. He admired her swan neck and her raven hair but he also liked her rapid mind and her "new" ideas; he was the very lover of her dreams. Though quite aware that he commanded Grace's affection, so the gossip ran, he offered his hand to another and, one supposes, a more brilliant *partie*. We have no exact dates for the courtship but rumor says that when the heiress rejected him he turned back to Miss Clarke. They were married on October 17, 1853, shortly after her return from Europe.

Strong-minded woman that she was Grace Greenwood is entirely of her period in her reticence about her personal affairs. Of her married life she wrote nothing at all. The Letters and the Leaves make frequent reference to her mother, her brothers, and her daughter but the word husband only occasionally occurs. There is almost no printed indication of Lippincott's part in her life.

For the explanation one is obliged to turn to a paragraph of newspaper gossip, written in 1876 when Leander Lippincott's peccadillos had swollen into crimes and he had fled the country under federal indictment. A Washington correspondent of the Hartford *Times* told the story of their marriage.

[Grace Greenwood's] dream of happiness was soon over, and her friends with indignation beheld the spectacle of her husband using all of her earnings for his own selfish pleasure. Loving, patient Grace, worked for both until proof after proof of his infidelities had been forced upon her. She entered the lecture field, and finally settled down in Washington as correspondent of the *New York Times*. Mr. Lippincott followed her to Washington and she obtained a clerkship for him in her brother's (Mr. Clarke's) office. Mr. Clarke is one of the examiners in the Patent Office. No one supposes that Mr. Lippincott made any better clerk than he did husband, or anything else.

Of this situation Grace Greenwood's Letters give no hint. Yet, for all her careful reticence, she has left us a record of her unsatisfactory marriage almost as clear and plain as the account of hers Jane Swisshelm set down in her unconventional autobiography. Her emotional experience Grace Greenwood turned into a story, the most romantic and elaborate she ever wrote.

"Zelma's Vow" appeared in the *Atlantic* (June and September, 1859). All contributions were then anonymous and the historical dress and melodramatic climax undoubtedly concealed from contemporary readers the autobiographical elements in the tale; but set side by side "Zelma's Vow" and that paragraph from the Hartford *Times* and it is difficult to avoid the inference that they are first- and third-person versions of the same story.

The Greenwood fiction had begun with fluffy little Heart Histories concocted for *Godey's* and *Graham's*. These expanded into novelettes which the *Saturday Evening Post* announced, months in advance, with pride. The Greenwood name had sales value, but that was probably not the only reason why James Russell Lowell thought it worth while to publish "Zelma's Vow" beside "The Professor at the Breakfast Table" and "The Minister's Wooing." Under the clichés and the contrived situations is an interesting and original theme: the artistic and emotional life of an eighteenth-century actress who disdains the conventions of her day and moves towards the "sublimity," the "instinct and inspiration of Nature" of a Mrs. Siddons. There is more than a touch of autobiography here; Sara Clarke had seriously considered the stage as a career.

Far removed from current stock characters is the leading masculine figure in the tale, "Lawrence Bury," who is neither villain nor hero but a dashing second-rate artist. He has some affinities with the "Anzoleto" of George Sand's *Consuelo*, which Grace Greenwood, like the other radicals of her generation, admired extravagantly, but his prototype, one feels constrained to believe, was Leander Lippincott.

He was a handsome, shapely person, with an assured, dashing manner, and a great amount of spirit and fire, which usually passed with his audience, and always with himself, for genius. His voice was powerful and resonant, his elocution effective, if not faultless, and his physical energy inexhaustible. Understanding and managing perfectly his own resources, he produced upon most provincial critics the impression of extraordinary power and promise, few perceiving that he had already come into full possession of his dramatic gifts. Only finely-trained ears could discover in this sounding, shining metal the lack of the sharp, musical ring of the genuine coin.

Zelma, a romanticized Grace, tall, dark, passionate, is the daughter of a reckless young soldier and his Spanish gypsy bride. She falls in love with the handsome strolling player and runs away with him, leaving the kind but narrowly conventional country gentry household of the uncle who has brought her up.

Her happiness is brief. The actor's "pettiness and egoism" soon begin to show. When finally, against his desire, Zelma tries her skill upon the stage and makes an instant London success, he is moved to a vindictive professional jealousy which stifles her love.

From that time Zelma went her own ways, calm and self-reliant outwardly, but inwardly tortured with a host of womanly griefs and regrets, a helpless sense of wrong and desolation. She flew to her beautiful art for consolation, flinging herself, with a sort of desperate abandonment, out of her own life of monotonous misery into the varied sorrows of the characters she personated.

Finally Bury leaves her for a tour of the provinces, "accompanied by the fair actress with whom he played first parts at Arden,—but now, green-room gossip said, not in a merely professional association." Then comes his death and, many years later, Zelma's own when she finds herself, in a small provincial town, playing the last act of *The Fair Penitent* with a skull which proves to be her husband's.

What impresses one most in this welter of sentiment

and melodrama is the indication that Grace Greenwood did not romanticize her own misjudgment of character but admitted it to herself fairly. She really had that strong-minded feminine pride about which she used to preach in her little stories of love and courtship and in her poems. Her most elaborate expression of it in "Ariadne" was admiringly reprinted again and again by the collectors of gems from the female poets. To the forsaken Princess of Crete, crying out in despair as she watches the receding sails of the faithless Theseus, Grace Greenwood speaks sternly thus:

> Worthy thou
> Of the dark fate which meets thee now,
> For thou art grovelling in thy woe;
> Arouse thee! joy to bid him go!
> For god above, or man below,
> Whose love's warm and impetuous tide
> Cold interest or selfish pride
> Can chill, or stay, or turn aside,
> Is all too poor and slight a thing
> One shade o'er woman's brow to fling
> Of grief, regret, or fear,—

This, said Mrs. Sarah Josepha Hale, reprinting it in *Eminent Women from the Creation to 1852*, is a new note.

Like Zelma, Grace Greenwood was a better practitioner of her "art" than her husband. It was her name on the masthead and the tales she wrote for its pages which made their joint publishing venture *The Little Pilgrim* one of the most popular juvenile magazines in the country. "It is not by imitating, but by reproducing childhood," declared Margaret Fuller, "that the writer becomes its companion," and that was precisely what Grace Greenwood did. She had a vivid memory for the details of her youthful adventures and recounted them with the same pleasure she found in sharing her adult experiences. "A Night in the Woods," for instance (March, 1866), describes a visit to the family maple sugar camp where, in the sap season, her brother and the hired man had to keep watch all night while the syrup boiled. Little Grace (Sara Jane she was then) persuaded her mother to let her undertake the daring adventure of spending a night with them by urging that "It's best to be prepared for everything. I may have to marry a missionary to the Indies." The sugar-making process is simply and clearly described while the narrative moves briskly from one amusing incident to the next, mixing entertainment with instruction in the best twentieth-century manner.

The Little Pilgrim himself is a charming figure as, in a woodcut on the cover, he mounts, tall staff in hand, a steep defile. Great rustic letters beneath announce Grace Greenwood's editorship. The well-designed pages are a pleasant mixture of story and verse under well-known signatures (the editor levied contributions from her literary friends on both sides of the water) with anecdotes and puzzles which the young readers and their parents were invited to supply. "We still have more enigmas sent us than we can possibly find room for," runs a plaintive note in the summer of 1863, "but none of our kind correspondents send us Charades or Rebuses of late. Will not some good friend lend us a helping hand in this line and oblige G.G."—whose weary initials are signed to most of the puzzles in this number as well as to numerous notes and stories.

Somewhat appalling to the twentieth-century parent is the column headed "Gone Home" which records touching deathbed scenes with young heads resting on snowy pillows smoothed by tender hands. There are poems, too, with such titles as "The Grave of the Twins," and letters from bereaved mothers telling how they wept when the last number of *The Little Pilgrim* arrived because a curly-haired six-year-old would never read it any more. These lugubrious sentimentalities furnished, apparently, for the nineteenth-century darling the vitamins which the atomic age infant imbibes in his bedtime meal of gangsters, cowboys, and supermen.

The Little Pilgrim was planned even before the Lippincotts' marriage and began his journey in November, 1853. Leander Lippincott seems to have undertaken the business management; they both worked at the editing; and Grace wrote stories or sketches for most of the numbers. Some of these, restewings of her European trip, Ticknor and Fields collected at the end of each year into attractively illustrated little volumes: *Merrie England, Bonnie Scotland, Stories and Sights of France and Italy, Stories and Legends of Travel, Stories of Many Lands*. She also continued to turn out Letters, novelettes, and sketches for the *Post* which liked to advertise that her "brilliant pen" would be exclusively employed in their service. But after the arrival of little Annie—the only child who lived—this did not quite suffice and Mrs. Lippincott made the bold decision to become a lecturer.

As a literary lady giving readings she was considerably more respectable than such unsexed reformers as Mrs. Swisshelm and Mrs. Bloomer; yet, to mount a platform was, in the 'fifties, a strong-minded proceeding and, knowing that many of her public would disapprove, she forestalled their strictures, a device she used often with success.

"Murder will out" [she wrote the *Post*, February 5, 1859], and as the papers have told you of the crime I have committed against the good old fashioned ideas of woman's place and mission, in "going out of my *spere* to *lectur*," as a worthy old gentlemen said of one of my predecessors—I suppose I may as well put a bold face on the matter myself. What is done, is *done*. The Rubicon of feminine reserve [one is reminded of Mrs. Swisshelm's Red Sea] is passed—if I do not go forward I cannot go back—henceforth I must be an object for the dainty horror of fine ladies—for the stale jokes of fine gentlemen—and an abomination to all Christian Turks.

She added that she had just met in Cleveland a large, kind, and encouraging audience.

Her audiences continued to be large and kind. She had a good voice and presence and a dramatic power that pleased a generation delighting in oratory. Soon she had all the engagements she could fill, many of them in the West where newborn lyceums were looking eagerly for culture.

For Grace Greenwood herself this treading of the boards was very pleasant, the partial fulfillment of an old dream. In her twenties she had seriously considered devoting her talents to acting and her numerous theatrical friends—closest of them was Charlotte Cushman—thought that she should. But her otherwise liberal family were opposed and, as she frankly admitted, she "never had a will strong enough to resist those she loved." But she kept a continual interest in the theater, filled many of her Letters with extended criticisms of plays and actors, and welcomed the opportunities the lyceum stage offered her for testing her theories of voice and gesture.

Yet whatever advantages it might have, the life of the lady lecturer was not an easy one, especially in the West. There she traveled often not far behind the covered wagon. Mrs. Swisshelm, touring Minnesota in the 'fifties, frequently covered the distance between engagements "in an open cutter, through a driving snow storm." Mrs. Bloomer kept an appointment in Nebraska by crossing an ice-filled river in a small boat. Mrs. Stanton writes cheerfully of "despicable hotels" and of sleeping on a station bench while waiting till four in the morning for a late train. Grace Greenwood, telling the tale of a journey in the caboose of a freight train—whose Irish crew were distressed when they found that their pipe smoke made her sick—remarks that she had already made trips on locomotives and handcars.

To the believer in the millennium, nevertheless, it was exciting to see a new world burgeoning and to help it with her "message." Most famous of the Greenwood messages was "The Heroic in Common Life," which moved the inmates of the Ohio State Penitentiary and the First Division of the Second Corps of the Union Army as well as more conventional lecture audiences.

The tours would have continued longer if little Annie had not begun adding to her evening prayer a petition "to the effect that folks should be restrained from sending for her mamma to come and lecture. She repeated that prayer so persistently, and with such fervent faith, that it finally prevailed, and the Lecture Committee never knew what did it."

Even a daughter of the Huguenots and Puritans might have felt justified in confining the lectures and Letters that supported a husband and daughter to topics which would arouse no controversy, which could be counted on to please. But Grace Greenwood was more than a literary lady; she was a propagandist who felt her power as an obligation. If she could help to improve the world, she must. If her literary "fame" could induce people to pay attention to her opinions then she must speak out what she believed. She was not a reformer in the usual nineteenth-century sense of the word; she did not attach herself to any particular cause, but the abolitionists and the suffragists, the pacifists and the opponents of capital punishment counted her always as a strong support, a spokesman with a special kind of force, for her propaganda insinuated itself into the consciousness of readers of the *Tribune*, the *Times*, and the *Post*, who would never have thought of subscribing to a reform journal. A pretty picture of autumn in the Pennsylvania hills, for instance, dissolves into a proposal for a reform of woman's dress so that she may benefit from country rambles. "City Sights and Thoughts," a series written for the *Post*, has column after column on the Asylum for Idiots in Columbus, Ohio, the Philadelphia Rosine Association for the rescue of Magdalens, or the Society for Alleviating the Miseries of Public Prisons. A glowing account of the rising city of Denver is interrupted by the statement that its county jail is "the darkest, foulest, most dreadful and disgusting hole in which I ever saw human beings penned and packed." Absorbed in a description of a visit to the Treasury Building in Washington the unwary reader finds himself entering a room where "some very pretty girls" are at work, "and it is cheering to a philanthropist to know that they are getting nearly as much as ordinary-looking young men would get for the same work, while it is comforting to a political economist to reflect how much during the ten years past Uncle Samuel has saved by employing women instead of men."

Even the Little Pilgrim carried propaganda in his script. When G.G. composes a rhymed charade on so innocuous a word as whippoorwill, "my first" becomes something the driver wields in the snowy cotton fields though

> fast comes on the day that ends
> Its reign of blood and fear—
> Comes with the sound of breaking chains,
> And the freedman's joyous cheer.

To the war for the preservation of the Union and the freedom of the slave Grace Greenwood gave her untiring support. She visited hospitals; she lectured for groups who were trying to raise funds to buy medical supplies and comforts for the army; she was a generous contributor to those interesting short-lived little journals published by the Sanitary Fairs. Ingenious devices for extracting yet a little more money from the pockets of a patriotic public, their fragile surviving pages demonstrate the commercial acumen, hitherto unsuspected, of the sheltered females whom war released into the business world.

The great fairs, organized in one city after another, lasted a week, ten days, even more. Each morning the committee in charge published a little newspaper, called by some appropriate title: *The Haversack*, *The Broken Fetter*, *The Spirit of the Fair*. It contained programs of the day's special events and exhibitions, announcements

Union Avenue at the Great Central Fair held in Philadelphia
in June, 1864, as pictured in *Our Daily Fare*, the newspaper of
the Exhibition

of the winners of lotteries, and also poems, stories, patriotic essays by writers well known to the readers of the better magazines. Each contribution, the editors took care to announce, was written especially for their pages. Grace Greenwood wrote of the solemn enthusiasm with which the declaration of war was received in Philadelphia, that city which had sent back to their masters so many fugitive slaves. She set down "A Few Plain Words" to English friends inclined to sympathize with the South. She eulogized the heroic death of Colonel Robert Shaw, "buried with his niggers." She rebuked the complacency of the Church towards the peculiar institution. President Lincoln, who had admired her Letters in the *Era*, seems to have followed with some attention her wartime writing and lecturing and is popularly reported to have called her "Grace Greenwood the Patriot."

What she thought of Lincoln she set down at some length. Twice she met him face to face. The first occasion was the White House reception in honor of General Tom Thumb and his bride. The irrepressible Barnum had proposed the affair and Mr. and Mrs. Lincoln with an amiable desire, so Grace Greenwood felt, to share a novel little entertainment with their friends, had sent out a limited number of invitations to those not likely to think such a ceremony undignified in a time of war. A good many of the press were invited and Grace was delighted to be received by the Lincolns as an old friend. They read both the *Era* and the *Post* and, in the Springfield days, their children had enjoyed *The Little Pilgrim*.

Mr. Lincoln [she says] before I heard his sweet-toned voice, and saw his singularly sympathetic smile, was certainly an awesome personage to me. So tall, gaunt and angular was his figure—so beyond all question plain, was his face, furrowed and harrowed by unexampled cares and infinite perplexities, while over all was a simple dignity which was more than sacerdotal—a peculiar, set-apart look, which I have never seen in any other man, never shall see.

The reception of the curious midget couple in the East Room Grace Greenwood found a trifle bizarre, yet

It was pleasant to see their tall host bend, and bend, to take their little hands in his great palm, holding Madame's with especial chariness, as tho it were a robin's egg, and he were fearful of breaking it. Yet he did not *talk* down to them, but made them feel from the first as tho he regarded them as real "folks," sensible, and knowing a good deal of the world.

Her second meeting was a year later when she took her little daughter, who wanted to see the President, to the last reception of the season. Lincoln welcomed Grace Greenwood cordially and was so touched by little Annie's look of reverence, as she shook his hand, that he bent down and kissed her.

The most unusual of Grace Greenwood's war experiences occurred in 1864. It began with a letter which seemed to her so singular that she reprinted it in full in a long sketch which she called "A Taste of Camp Life."

Dear Madam:—Will it be agreeable and possible for you to give some lectures this season before the Lecture Association of the First Division (General Caldwell's), Second Army Corps? We have a fine hall, built for this purpose, and have a number of distinguished gentlemen engaged for the course. There are now a large number of ladies visiting in the division, and you could not fail to be interested, as well as to interest, should you accept our invitation. . . . It is the desire of

the officers, ladies, and men of this command, as well as of
the society, that your services may be secured for one, two,
or three evenings.

Of course she went, taking little Annie with her and escorted by one of her brothers. Passes from the War Department were necessary and the trip through war-torn
Virginia was made by narrow gauge and ambulance. The
lecturer was greeted by the regimental band, entertained
by the General, and found among the hardships of camp
life "(tell it not to Grant! publish it not in the Tribune!)
a veritable *feather-bed*, with feather pillows." She had
stage fright before her first lecture but the audience proved
to be "kindly demonstrative and inspiring. They received
the patriotic passages with loyal applause; they 'laughed
at little jests' with the most benignant good-humor; and
they only did not weep over the pathetic pictures, because, as soldiers, they couldn't consistently do so much
for me."

She lectured again to the officers and repeated her first
lecture to the enlisted men.

Never did I have a more courteous and attentive audience.
There was in the lecture a strong radical element; there were
ideas that must have seemed to many of them novel and
startling, points on which they must have disagreed with me;
but not one word or movement of displeasure or dissent did
they give. They heard me out calmly and most good-
humoredly. . . .

It was a strange experiment, which, I venture to say, could
be successfully tried with the private soldiers of no other
army in the world. Fancy Wellington's beef-eaters or Ennis-
killeners listening for an hour and a quarter to Maria Edgeworth or Hannah More.

Next day there was an alarm—a party of Rebels had crossed the Rapidan, but they retired without action and the visitors finished in safety their agreeable week in camp.

The cause to which Grace Greenwood turned her valiant pen after the slaves were free and the Union whole again was one to which few of her readers could take exception: she tried to make the Easterner understand the West, visit and explore it, take up land and help in the building of a new earth. "Were I a man," she wrote from Greeley, Colorado, "I would rather give my name to a town like this, and teach such a brave colony what I knew of farming, than be President of the United States."

About Colorado and the rest of the West she knew more than most women, or for the matter of that men, of her generation. New Brighton, which was near Pittsburgh, counted as West in those days, but the Clarke brothers and sisters had gone further on, to Ohio, Michigan, Iowa, and soon after their marriage the Lippincotts were spending summers with relatives on the Middle Border. Lecture tours and visits took Mrs. Lippincott through the Ohio Valley, to Chicago, Kansas, Utah, Nevada, even to San Francisco. But her special land of promise was Colorado, partly because of the romantic grandeur of the Rockies—quite as impressive as Switzerland; partly because in the high dry air she found at last real relief from her torturing asthma. "As for confirmed asthmatics, . . . they who once a year at least must rehearse the death-agony, yet cannot die,—for them, brothers and sisters in affliction, I have to say that I do not believe there is out of Heaven such a place as the mountain land of Colorado."

Again and again she went back for summer "rambles" and finally cemented her allegiance by taking up an acre and a half of land. Colorado's right to statehood became in consequence one of the themes of her Washington Letters to the *Times*. When it was denied in 1873, she taxed her imagination for adequate curses on the impercipient senators: "Ha! may they all be left by the train, over night, at Greeley, each man with an empty pocket flask, and not a euchre deck about him."

Colorado appreciated her value as a publicity agent. Railroad presidents invited her to travel in their private cars; governors guided her on trips to distant canyons. A "knob" in the Caribou Mine was named after her. The officials of the Denver and Rio Grande insisted that she drive with her own hands a spike in their narrow-gauge road. She was invited to the opening of the government weather station on Pike's Peak, and cooked flapjacks for the whole party when other provisions failed to arrive. Elizabeth Greatorex, for whose book of Colorado etchings she wrote an introduction, gives an account of a camping trip during which one of the carriages was overturned in a gulch and the passengers thrown out on the rocks. Bruised, cut, and shaken they managed to reach a little hotel where Mrs. Lippincott fainted from exhaustion. The proprietress, rushing in with restoratives, stopped to cry out with pleasure: "Oh! What an honor to have Grace Greenwood faint on my floor."

The *Times* Letters of 1871 and 1872 spread their propaganda still further when they were collected into a book, *New Life in New Lands*. "Grace," wrote a reviewer in the Buffalo *Express*, "always finds lots of things no one else would see; and she has a happy knack of picking up the mountains and cities and big trees, and tossing them across the continent right before the reader's eyes. It's very convenient."

The Letters have a proper romantic enthusiasm for scenery but Grace Greenwood was even more interested in the inhabitants of the new country, both the settlers and the Indians who were still a major problem. Like Jane Swisshelm she looks at Indians with the eyes of a pioneer rather than of an Eastern humanitarian. In *New Life in New Lands*, for example, she tells of the landlady of a hotel in Golden, Colorado, who was once a passenger on a stagecoach attacked on the plains by "a band of chivalrous Cheyennes. She escaped, with several arrows sticking in her arms and shoulders. These romantic mementos, these primitive relics, should doubtless have prompted her and her friends to deal gently with the erring red man, but I don't think they did."

"Though I want the peace policy thoroughly tried," runs a Letter to the *Times* from Washington in January, 1873, "to the satisfaction of the Administration and the Quakers, I must confess that I am a sad infidel, with regard to the regeneration of the red man. I am only orthodox enough to believe in aboriginal sin."

The wretched story of Leander Lippincott came to an end, so far as we have any record, in April, 1876. He was then chief clerk of the General Land Office of the Department of the Interior. An important part of his duty was the recording of claims for the Chippewa Indians in Minnesota to whom the government was issuing script for four hundred acres of land apiece. The opportunity for skillful chicanery was too tempting. Working with a few accomplices Lippincott succeeded in collecting at least $25,000 as fees for passing fraudulent claims, and apparently amassed some other loot as well. When the government discovered what was going on he stoutly denied all charges and there seemed to be no way of proving his guilt until the authorities unearthed a disgruntled member of his band who, when he broke with the others, had carried off an incriminating collection of letters and documents. Under this evidence Lippincott confessed and was indicted by the Grand Jury, but before he could be arrested he fled the country. That is the last we know of him, except the fact that a Washington correspondent, sending an account of the scandal to the Detroit *News*, described the absconder as "one of the most accomplished, witty, genial and intelligent gentlemen in the public service."

Mrs. Lippincott was in Paris at the time. She had gone abroad in the autumn of 1875 with Annie and another "unprotected female," sojourning in England, Switzerland, and France, reporting her explorations in long letters to the *Times*. One of these budgets went off almost every week, except in April when there was a long silence, explained later as due to illness. To friends she wrote that she believed the charges against her husband false.

In 1877 Mrs. Lippincott and her daughter returned to America. A year or so later they went abroad again to continue the musical education of Annie who had a clear high soprano voice, a charming unaffected stage manner, and, apparently, a very fair degree of talent. She studied singing in London, Paris, and Milan, chaperoned always by her mother, who wrote for the *Independent* some interesting and informative articles on the opportunities and dangers that await in Europe the aspiring young American musician. They are in the best Greenwood vein, filled with firsthand information, speaking out plainly without respect of persons. "In this article I have let a lot of cats out of the bag. I hope none of them will turn and rend me."

Comment on current political and literary affairs Grace Greenwood sent to the *Independent* also whenever some particularly interesting event moved her to expression. She was reading constantly English, French, and Italian newspapers and she went, with the indefatigable energy of a true journalist, to observe at firsthand anything that stirred her curiosity, from the liquefaction of the blood of San Carlo of Milan to the teaching methods of a famous singer. She reports on the cholera epidemic in Toulon with a discussion of what medical science knows about the cause and prevention of the plague; gives an account of the Communist demonstrations in Paris on the anniversary of the death of Blanqui; writes an obituary of Garibaldi, with vivid personal recollections of an interview he granted her in Rome in 1876; describes the rejoicing in Paris over the reduction of the duty on works of art imported into the United States, adding an account of the generous opportunities offered to American artists by the French Government. She is doing propaganda here for a cause she had always much at heart: the free international circulation of "those fair ministers of civilization," works of art.

All these articles are good reading today. Through

years of practice in writing Grace Greenwood had learned at last to write. She no longer puts down every notion that flits through her head; she can be enthusiastic without superlatives; she is not now led astray into merely verbal puns; she does not gush; but she has not lost with age her enthusiastic curiosity, her fresh delight in the new thing, nor her desire to share an experience. She never lost either the compulsion to bear witness to her principles in and out of season.

An amusing example of this propensity is the little book she wrote during these years abroad and published simultaneously in London and New York. *Queen Victoria, Her Girlhood and Womanhood* presents the Queen to American girls as an ennobling example of wife and mother. Gliding lightly over politics it concentrates on family relationships, travels about the kingdom, and picturesque state ceremonies, used, all of them, as settings for the display of a strong and interesting personality. The portrait which emerges is engaging; Her Majesty herself commended it. But for all her admiration Grace Greenwood speaks as an American and a republican.

I could not do otherwise; for though it [this study] has made me in love with a few royal people, it has not made me in love with royalty. . . . It suits England . . . "excellently well," in its restricted form . . . but it would not do for us, . . . To us it seems, though a primitive, an unnatural institution. We find no analogies for it, even in the wildest venture of the New World. It is true the buffalo herd has its kingly commander . . . ; the drove of wild horses has its chieftain . . . ; even the migratory multitudes of wild-fowl . . . have their general and engineer,—but none of these leaders was born or hatched into his proud position.

They are undoubtedly chosen, elected, or elect themselves by superior will or wisdom. Entomology does, indeed, furnish some analogies. The sagacious bees, the valiant wasps, are monarchists,—but then, they have only Queens.

Towards the end of the 'eighties mother and daughter came back to the United States, probably because of Annie's approaching marriage. Grace Greenwood settled for a time in New York and then, in 1892, took a house in Washington, 218 New Jersey Avenue, within easy distance of the Capitol. There, at seventy, she began to write for the *Independent* a series of "Reminiscences of Washington Before and During the War." As lively as the Letters of the 'fifties and very much better reading, these articles are by no means the work of a woman living in her past. They carry pertinent comment on the passing scene and strike, again and again, sharp blows for good causes not yet quite won.

August 14, 1902:—If, as some of us who remember the old times fear, we are lazily drifting toward another era of Southern dictation and Northern acquiescence, a state of things likely to be disagreeable and discreditable to both sections, it seems to me that next to the old race prejudice, strangely acerbated, and a gross and grasping commercialism, the popular light literature of the day, mostly of Northern authorship, may be responsible for such a misfortune, such harm to our national character. For some years past magazine stories and historical novels, so called, have been given to extravagant if not invidious glorifications of Southern men and manners, Southern heroism, honor and hospitality, feudality, beauty, chivalry, blue blood, blue grass, and all that. Such literature is marked by a namby-pamby magnanimity which is not acceptable to the proud South, and which is the essence of disloyalty to the North.

A serious illness interrupted these reminiscences for a time but Grace Greenwood resumed them from her daughter's home in New Rochelle, New York. She wrote the last one only a few months before she died, April 20, 1904, at the age of eighty-one.

THE LITTLE PILGRIM.

EDITED BY

Grace Greenwood.

PHILADELPHIA.

MARCH, 1866

Louisa S. McCord, a bust by Hiram Powers

Altogether Doric

LOUISA S. McCORD

THE bust that Hiram Powers modeled suggests the head of a Roman matron. The verse tragedy which brought her poetic fame had for its hero Caius Gracchus; she dedicated it to her only son and certainly she saw herself in the role of Cornelia. "Her mind," wrote J. W. Davidson in his *Living Writers of the South* (1869), "is Roman in its cast, and heroic in its energy"; in person, intellect, and character, he added, she is "altogether *Doric*."

Doric and Roman were Southern euphemisms for strong-minded, a term never applied to a lady below the Mason-Dixon Line. Louisa Cheves McCord was proud to be known as intellectual and literary and she wanted to improve the world but she permitted no one to class her with Grace Greenwood and Antoinette Brown. She knew the role that God had designed for woman and it was not that of reformer. Louisa Cheves' father, whom she admired this side idolatry, had traced for her the divine plan and she gloried in adapting herself, however keen the sacrifice, to her appointed position in the pattern.

Her other basic principles she took also from her father, but not by rote; she battled her way through to them for herself, sharpening new arguments and erecting stronger fortifications as she went along. To hasten the millennium she panted as ardently as though she breathed the air of New England or New York. Every American in that golden day believed that, under the direction of God and Nature, the world was growing better. It was the human task to push it on, at the proper speed, along the path of progress. But which was the path and what the proper speed? There were the points of conflict. The reforms her Northern sisters labored for seemed to Louisa Cheves a mad driving of swine to the brink of the cliff. The strong-minded women, she thought, not content to follow the divine timetable, were rushing on by a schedule of their own and, in their haste, had utterly lost the way. It was her mission to show them the error in their course, to point the true path along which the world should move, to demonstrate the fanatical illogic of Fourierism, communism, protective tariffs, abolition, woman's rights, and bloomers.

Louisa Cheves (Chĭvĭs) resembled her distinguished father as well as admiring him. She had the excellent mind, the physical energy, and the imperious disposition which made him, at sixteen a penniless, uneducated clerk, president, at forty, of the Bank of the United States. O'Neal, in his *Bench and Bar of South Carolina* (1859), said that if Langdon Cheves had remained in Congress he would have been President of the United States. The portrait in Governor Benjamin Perry's *Reminiscences of Public Men* is equally laudatory though rather more informal. Cheves' daughter thought it lacking in respect and wrote an angry correction for the *Nineteenth Century* where the *Reminiscences* first appeared. She questioned, too, some of the governor's facts about her father's youthful poverty and her grandfather's toryism. Since she had never heard these stories, she said, it was unlikely that they were true. Fortunately the twentieth-century members of the family have, with historical objectivity, confirmed and enlarged them. They make a good American tale.

Langdon Cheves' father, Alexander, migrated to America from Aberdeenshire in 1762. Twenty-one, shrewd, hardy, and adventurous, he became a successful trader to the Cherokees and Creeks on the South Carolina frontier. In 1774 he married Mary Langdon of Virginia and their only child, Langdon, was born, 1776, in Bull Town Fort in the Abbeville district where his mother had taken refuge against an attack by hostile Indians.

Alexander Cheves was by inclination loyal to the King but the Colonies forced him to take their oath of allegiance and to do military duty, though he managed to restrict his army service to the driving of provision wagons. He urged this proof of his true sentiments when he went to England at the end of the war to make application for relief as a loyalist who had lost property for his devotion to the Crown, but His Majesty's Commissioners found his colonial oath against him and he got no money by his journey. He did, though, find in Scotland a second wife— Langdon's mother had died in 1779—with whom he returned to Charlestown and opened a store on Sullivan's Island.

Young Langdon, who did not get on with his stepmother, decided to make himself independent. He found a position with a factor where he acquired the beautiful handwriting for which he was always famous and a skill in tying up bundles and sanding floors of which he liked to boast, in the Sir Joseph Porter manner, in later life. By the time he was sixteen he had proved himself so efficient and trustworthy that his employer sent him out in charge of boatloads of supplies to the plantations with which the firm did business.

Cheves' legal vocation began, according to the legend, when, passing one day by the Charleston Courthouse, he stopped to listen to the resonant voice of Chancellor William Marshall arguing a case. Though he had scarcely any schooling the boy decided then and there to become a lawyer. He borrowed books and studied after working hours and, a few years later, asked Judge Marshall to let him read law in his office. When he was twenty-one he was admitted to the bar.

At first his practice was limited, for he declined any cases in which he could not thoroughly believe, but by the time he was thirty he had the most lucrative practice ever known in South Carolina. He and his partner were said to divide $20,000 a year. In 1808 he was made attorney general of the state and two years later went to Washington as a member of the House of Representatives. With his great head—"the largest head of any public man in America"—broad forehead, and full red face, he was an impressive figure when he rose to speak in thundering periods which reminded Washington Irving of Cicero and Demosthenes. Yet Langdon Cheves never, till late in life, set pen to paper without trepidation, so conscious was he of his deficient education. That his daughter became famous for her ability to transmute the family energy into powerful prose was a strong vicarious satisfaction.

Langdon Cheves' attitude toward England was very different from that of his father. With Clay, Calhoun, Lowndes, and Bibb, he formed in Washington the "War

Mess" who defied Britain to conflict in 1812. His admirers called him, in consequence, the Father of the United States Navy. Meanwhile he was acquiring property in South Carolina and becoming more and more dominant as a social as well as a political figure. He married, in 1806, Miss Mary Elizabeth Dulles of Charleston, one of those innumerable ladies of whom the story is told that when a careless slave overturned a tureen of soup on her blue brocade gown she did not even interrupt the remark she was addressing to her dinner partner.

Of their fourteen children the two eldest sons were reckless and charming. They drank and gamed and dueled and came to untimely ends. The others—one would like to know just what change took place in the tactics of parental control—were all estimable citizens. Two of them, Langdon, Junior, and John, had inventive and mechanical gifts which made them good rice planters and useful engineers in the Confederate army. Langdon, Junior, became famous as a builder of fortifications and the designer and operator of the Confederate army's only observation balloon. The eldest daughter, Sophia, was described by her friends as wise, calm, and brave. Louisa Susannah, younger by a year—she was born December 3, 1810—was sometimes wise and always brave but seldom calm.

In 1815 Langdon Cheves' friends in Washington were talking about him for the presidency but, believing his national service accomplished, he declined the secretaryship of the Treasury and returned to his Charleston law practice. A year later he was elected justice of the Court of Appeals and in 1819 Monroe selected him for the Supreme bench but he was persuaded, as a patriotic duty, to accept instead the presidency of the Bank of the United States, then in such parlous health that its life was despaired of. With sound judgment and courage Cheves administered two drastic remedies: a sharp curtailment of circulation and a European loan. He made thereby many enemies but within a few years the Bank was sound and firm. Cheves had saddled the horse, it was said, for Nick Biddle to ride.

Direction of the Bank required residence in Philadelphia so the Cheves daughters, ten and nine years old, had their first formal schooling at the North, and the Judge saw to it that it was the best the city had to offer. They went first to the academy conducted by an accomplished Irishman, Mr. Grimshaw, and were then placed under the tutelage of two refugees, M. and Mme. Picot, who made them really proficient in French and taught them also a little Italian. But Louisa's active mind was not satisfied with even this superior female nutriment. She was discovered one day hiding behind the door of the room where her brothers' tutor was expounding mathematics. She was scribbling down the problems he dictated on a bit of paper and trying to solve them. Her father was impressed and pleased. Here was a repetition of his own early struggle for an education. Louisa, he said, should be taught anything she cared to learn. She did her mathematics in future with the door open and plunged with her brothers into the classics.

It was at Mr. Grimshaw's academy that Louisa first encountered the slavery problem. Her new schoolmates accused her of coming from the South and then assured her that they knew all about the way plantation owners treat their Negroes. "Father's cousin's wife's sister" had been at the South once and she had discovered that the

Negroes are fed on cottonseed and have padlocks put on their mouths to keep them from eating corn while they are in the fields. Little Louisa struggled to refute these monstrous fictions, in vain. They had, the young Yankees insisted, the facts, and the sense of helpless frustration she experienced as she tried to convince them of the real truth of the matter stayed with her all her life.

Truly it would seem [she wrote thirty years later reviewing *Uncle Tom's Cabin* for the *Southern Quarterly*] that the labour of Sisyphus is laid upon us, the slaveholders of these southern United States. Again and again have we, with all the power and talent of our clearest heads and strongest intellects, forced aside the foul load of slander and villainous aspersion so often hurled against us, and still, again and again, the unsightly mass rolls back, and, heavily as ever, fall the old refuted libels, vamped, remodeled, and lumbering down upon us with all the force, or at least impudent assumption, of new argument.

The abolitionists, Louisa Cheves always believed, were actuated chiefly by ignorance; a firsthand acquaintance with slavery would surely convince them of the error of their way.

The sisters went into society in Philadelphia and in Washington. They met, at their parents' dinner table, the influential statesmen of the day and listened to eloquent talk on finance and tariffs and states' rights. In 1829 Langdon Cheves turned the Bank of the United States over to Nicholas Biddle and took his family back to Charleston. The next year Sophia married and it was then, undoubtedly, that Louisa, just turned twenty, went through her great mental struggle on the position of woman.

What she must have longed to do was to go into politics.

She had, she knew very well, more than any other member of the family, the qualities of temperament and mind, the energy and courage, the fluency of speech, the readiness for battle which had made Langdon Cheves successful in the courtroom and the legislative halls. She had the education which he, at her age, had lacked. She had studied with her brothers and she knew that she was as good a man as any of them. Even her physique was masculine; to be tall and queenly with the head of a Roman matron was no asset to a young lady in Charleston. Her chances of making a sensation in Congress seemed a good deal better than her chances of cutting a swath on the ballroom floor or marrying promptly like Sophia. Her ambition, her restlessness, her deep discontent she poured out in poems which were later published as *My Dreams*. While she was composing them, they were read only by her sympathetic and admiring father. Unfortunately they are such bad poems, so platitudinous and abstract in their labored metaphors and diction, that we can gather, among the solid Doric violets and rainbows, no concrete details of the course of her feminist conflict. There is only the clear evidence of youthful unhappiness and thwarted ambition.

"The Comet"

> Hast thou no resting place, thou wandering thing?
> Art thou an emblem of the soul, which roams
> Eternally, and seeks a home and rest?

"The Firefly"

> What though thou, like me, must find—
> Born to Earth, doomed to regretting—
> Vainly that the restless mind
> Seeks to soar, its birth forgetting.

The pressure which kept Louisa Cheves in the straight path of true womanhood was both social and divine. The Southern states were as firmly directed as New England by a wise Providence which had assigned to each creature its particular sphere but while in the North the precise boundaries of that sphere were a matter of frequent controversy, in the Southern states they were clearly and firmly fixed. A more stable society with far more rigid class lines implemented the divine plan. Where the limits and duties of each race were so plainly marked it seemed logical that each sex should have its limits and its duties, and if the eternal pattern is sometimes constricting to the individual, yet it makes for general harmony and happiness. Woman's role is clearly defined:

> Her mission is
> To labour and to pray; to help, to heal,
> To soothe, to bear; patient with smiles to suffer.

That laborious program Louisa Cheves presented in "Woman's Progress," a long blank verse poem published in the *Southern Literary Messenger* in 1853. Two elaborate prose statements of her position on the woman's rights question she had made earlier, in the *Southern Quarterly*, April, 1852, and in *De Bow's Review* for September of the same year. They are written with so much passion that one feels certain these are the arguments with which she had subdued her own rebellious pride twenty years before. That women, American women, should struggle against the cosmic plan stirs her contemptuous anger:

"Woman was made for *duty*, not for *fame*; and so soon as she forgets this great law of her being, which consigns her to a life of heroism if she will—but quiet, unobtrusive heroism—she throws herself from her position, and thus, of necessity, degrades herself." The world might be improved by some alteration in the relative position of the sexes but "we have never allowed ourselves to speculate upon the propriety or impropriety of an arrangement, so evidently marked by the Almighty hand, that we have resigned ourselves to it as a fixed necessity."

The *Southern Quarterly* article was touched off by a report of the Proceedings of the Woman's Rights Convention held at Worcester, Massachusetts, in October, 1851, and an article by Harriet Martineau in the *Westminster*. The *De Bow's* discussion is a review of Mrs. E. Oakes Smith's *Woman and Her Needs*. Louisa Cheves had never of course met any suffragists in the flesh and her description of their minds is no more accurate than the abolitionist pictures of slavery to which she took such hot exception. Vanity was the only incentive by which she could imagine them to be pricked, vanity and misdirected energy. The cramping of talents, the legal constrictions and injustices which were so evident to Mrs. Bloomer and Mrs. Swisshelm she had never felt or witnessed. And, Louisa Cheves argued, even if injustice exists, woman's rights conventions and the ballot are not the way to remedy it. Women legislators would act only under authority delegated by man who could, at any moment, revoke that authority by virtue of his superior might. He has the physical right to rule and woman combats God's law when she rebels against man's power. Her sphere is higher, purer than man's; she is "designed by nature, the conservative power of the world." Woman must strive and pray while man strives and fights, forgetting often where wrath should cease and mercy rule; it is her task

to arrest the uplifted arm and whisper, "Peace, be still!"
Behind these fine axioms rises not only the great head of
Langdon Cheves but the figure of a lady in blue damask
keeping within bounds the hot words on nullification de-
claimed across the judicial dinner table.

Yet when she encounters a feminist issue on which
neither her parents nor her God have spoken, Louisa
Cheves' judgment is as straight and individual as Amelia
Bloomer's, though their conclusions seldom coincide. The
De Bow's article, for instance, carries an interesting foot-
note on the Bloomer costume:

We really mean nothing disrespectful of the dress, which,
as far as we know anything about it, is not only entirely un-
objectionable, but we decidedly think, from description, (we
have never ourselves been so happy as to encounter a real
live Bloomer,) a great improvement upon the dirty length of
skirt, wherewith our fashionables sweep the pavements and
clear off the ejected tobacco of our rail-road cars. The *dress*
is not only convenient, but entirely modest; and could the
same be said of its *wearers*, we would decidedly be of the
number of its advocates. We object to it, not as intrinsically
wrong in itself, but only in so far as it is used for wrong
purposes. . . . It is the rallying standard of woman's rights
advocates, and as such unfit for a modest female. Had it been
but the invention of some Parisian *modiste*, or some country,
field-tripping milk-maid, or of any other womanish thing,
imagined womanishly and worn womanishly, we would not
have hesitated to recommend it to our daughters. But indifferent things become vicious entirely by their uses; and the uses
to which the Bloomer dress have been applied condemn it
in toto.

At one other point Louisa Cheves almost agreed with
her Northern sisters: "There is nothing unwomanish in

the fullest exercise by woman of the thought and mind, which, if God has given, he has given for use. There is nothing unwomanish in the writing of such thoughts; nothing unwomanish even, we think, in the publishing of them." But, though God and society permit woman this liberty in the exercise of her literary power, she must remember that "it is *not her highest destiny. It is not her noblest life.*"

Another employment proper to woman was care for the welfare of the slaves on her estate, a duty which actually devolved upon Louisa Cheves in 1830 when she inherited from an aunt "Lang Syne" plantation in the cotton-raising "up-country" near Columbia. Sophia and her husband were settled in the same neighborhood and a letter from their mother reports on the girls' adaptation to their new responsibilities, especially their industry in making clothes for their "people." Louisa, who had never tried anything of the kind before, cut out and made up pantaloons and "Jackson" coats, finishing sometimes two coats in a day, and "the work will last as long as the cloth." She also made shirts and all the clothes for the women and children. And, with her father's advice one supposes, directed the business affairs of Lang Syne with determination and success.

Except for such occasional references as these the next decade of Louisa Cheves' life is without record. Her prose writing did not begin until after her marriage, at the advanced age of thirty, to David J. McCord of Columbia. His son, by his first marriage, had just formed an alliance with one of Louisa's nieces and the consequent family gatherings seem to have effected the second match.

"Handsome Davy" McCord was famous in the state for

his lively talk, his sound legal knowledge, and his hot Irish temper. Since he disapproved of dueling he always settled a difference on the spot with fists or cane and, despite his short stature, settled it usually to his own satisfaction.

Born in Columbia in 1797, David McCord attended South Carolina College and married at twenty the beautiful Emeline Wagner of Charleston. He began law practice in Columbia as the partner of Henry J. Nott whom he assisted in the editing of the decisions of the Constitutional Court of the state. Later he edited also the reports of the Court of Appeals. For five years he sat in the State Legislature. He was known as a bitter politician, ready to follow his principles to any extreme. He was editor of the Columbia *Telescope*, most violent of nullification papers, and when, in 1833, the Nullifiers determined to clinch their doctrine of state sovereignty by forcing all state officers to take the oath of allegiance, he undertook the disagreeable business from which his colleagues shrank. In 1837 he was made president of the Columbia branch of the State Bank, a position which he filled with competence for several years until his Whig principles made resignation necessary. As editor of the *Telescope*, and later, he worked closely with Jefferson's friend Dr. Thomas Cooper who sent him abroad, it was whispered, in 1830 to learn how much assistance South Carolina might expect from England in the event of secession. When Cooper, who was too radical for the University of Virginia where Jefferson wanted him, became president of South Carolina College, McCord interested himself in its development and served several times as a member of its board of trustees.

It was at about the time of his marriage to Louisa Cheves

that David McCord's retirement from the State Bank became necessary. He withdrew from active political life, though he continued to write political articles for the reviews, and devoted himself to the management of his wife's plantation in Abbeville and others which he and his brother owned in Alabama.

The years of her marriage, from 1840 to 1855 when David McCord died, were the happiest of Louisa McCord's life. Her three children were born in 1842, 1843, and 1845. Langdon Cheves, Harriet Cheves, and Louisa Rebecca Hayne. In the family memory Louisa McCord is written down as a devoted mother and stepmother who not only took pains with her children's upbringing but liked to share their amusements and games. There is a slightly grim note in the little tales that are told to support this character: how she once cut off the end of her long coil of black hair to make a tale for a rocking horse, and how she encouraged her offspring when it occurred to them to pitch out of a window Clark Mills' portrait bust of her which she disliked though her husband admired it.

The girls seem to have grown up as exemplary, pleasant young females submissively dominated by their mother but the son, Cheves, was an individual. The little portrait in the Confederate Museum in Richmond shows him erect and slender with a sensitive mouth and dark eyes that gaze into the distance, as though he foresaw his gallant youthful death. His mother believed that he would be as distinguished as the grandfather for whom he was named and her *Caius Gracchus*, written when he was ten years old, suggests that she dreamed of realizing in his person the political triumphs which her sex denied her.

Captain Cheves McCord, to whom his mother
dedicated her *Caius Gracchus*, a portrait in
the Confederate Museum, Richmond

That the political career she did have was quite as revolutionary as that of the most virulent Northern suffragist seems not to have been apparent to Louisa McCord. She was really a strong-minded woman though she did not shatter woman's sphere; she simply stretched it, into a new shape to be sure, but a shape respectably consistent with the divine plan. The propriety of her course was strengthened by the fact that it was her husband who initiated her unprecedented action.

The protective tariff which Northern manufacturers felt so important to their well-being and progress had long goaded the Southern planter to anger. Not only was it a burden to him; it was actually, would they only face the facts, a burden to the North as well. How to make the Northern states conscious of this truth was a perpetual problem to such legislators as Langdon Cheves and David McCord. When the distinguished French economist Frédéric Bastiat published his *Sophismes Economiques* they were delighted with its lucid exposition of the fundamental errors of the protective policy, an exposition quite as apposite for America as for France. They wished that American voters could be exposed to Bastiat's clear reason. Then it occurred to David McCord that his wife, thanks to her youthful training under M. and Mme. Picot, was an excellent French scholar. She was also, having listened to political discussions since she was ten, an informed political economist. Louisa McCord was delighted at the suggestion that she use her mind and skill in the Southern cause.

It was a daring venture for a Southern lady but as many guards as possible surrounded her name in its first appearance in print. *Sophisms of the Protective Policy*, the title page announced (1848), translated by Mrs. D. J. McCord of South Carolina. Then there was an Introductory Letter by Dr. Francis Lieber, Professor of Political Philosophy and Economy in South Carolina College, and another from "the subscriber," D. J. McCord, to the People of the United States: "This little volume is presented to your serious consideration. There is not one of you whom it does not materially concern."

Mrs. McCord's translation is clear, close, accurate, so accurate even that it is occasionally stiff and unidiomatic. Bastiat's meaning is always there if his manner occasionally escapes; the Roman hand is sometimes a little heavy on the Gallic irony.

David McCord's gift to the People of the United States was well received both North and South and when, a few months later, Bastiat published in the *Journal des Economistes* important essays on "Justice and Fraternity" and "The Right to Labor," Milton Clapp asked Mrs. McCord to review them for the *Southern Quarterly*. Articles signed L.S.M. appeared in July and October, 1849, and Louisa McCord was known henceforth as a literary lady, though her laurels were of a very different cut from those of the female poets and novelists the South was accustomed to admire. Fancy and imagination Carolina recognized as womanly gifts but propaganda, like oratory, was a masculine prerogative. No wonder people began to speak of Mrs. McCord as Roman.

Other editors followed the *Quarterly's* lead and L.S.M. was soon writing two or three long articles a year, on political economy, on the institution of slavery, on woman's rights. Sometimes her essay appears in the same issue with one by her husband, and always it is the more interesting of the two. O'Neal, in his *Bench and Bar*, says of David McCord that he had legal ingenuity but wanted force and point to impress a jury and was not infrequently tedious. The same qualities mark his writing, which is intelligent but dry while his wife's crackles with Langdon Cheves' oratorical fire:

Oh! there are things so fearful in their folly, terrific and yet comically mad, we laugh even when we shudder, in the gazing. "There is nothing more frightful than active ignorance." A Grace Greenwood, a Whittier, an Abby Folsom, a Thomson [sic], a Sumner or a Garrison, may, in their ignorant fanaticism, set the world on fire. They play with sheathed lightnings, careless at what moment these may burst from their confinement, to light the funeral pile of all that is good and great upon our earth. To point a stanza or a paragraph, they rouse nations to madness. Too late, in the sweeping desolation which must follow, will they see the evil of their ways. ("Negro and White Slavery—Wherein Do They Differ?" *Southern Quarterly Review*, July, 1851.)

Look, ladies, at the slave at your own door; the Lazarus at the gate of Dives. Though decorously excluded from the princely gates of Stafford-house, turn but a few corners and you will find the thronging multitudes of misery. Blind alleys are here, damp cellars, filthy garrets, the stench and the wretchedness and the vice of which are scarcely decent for the investigations of gentle ladies; hells, to which our poorest negro hut would present a cheerful and a blessed contrast. England, your own proud, happy England, teems with wretchedness. . . . ladies! even at your chariot wheels, almost under them, crushed in the dust and grovelling in their wretchedness, lie these, the victims of the juggernaut of English aristocracy. ("British Philanthropy and American Slavery," an Affectionate Response to the Ladies of England, etc., from the Ladies of the Southern United States," *De Bow's Review*, March, 1853.)

Perfect freedom is, we repeat, incompatible with society. *Equal* freedom, a freedom setting all men upon the same footing, has been dreamed of, has been talked of, but never seriously aimed at by any government. Does our own government, or did it at any period of its existence, or did its framers in any way, uphold so preposterous an idea? Miss Antoinette Brown, Sojourner Truth & Co., do talk of it; but no reasonable man, (we beg the ladies' pardon, we mean no exclusion of them, the term man, signifying with us, human being,) no reasoning individual ever imagined so anomalous a state of society. Mr. Jefferson's great humbug flourish of "free and equal," has made trouble enough, and it is full time that its mischievous influence should end. ("Carey on the Slave Trade," *Southern Quarterly Review*, January, 1854.)

Louisa McCord would probably have been effective on the platform but that unfeminine position now held no temptation. It was quite enough to set her great walnut writing table on the opposite side of the fireplace from her husband's, to use the books of reference in his legal library, to consult him now and then on the setting of an argument or the turning of a phrase, as he consulted her.

It was a good life. She had her family, her writing, and her plantation duties. Lang Syne, some thirty miles from Columbia, lay in the beautiful piney region where the trees grew so tall and free from underbrush that you could drive a carriage and pair among them and there was no need for bridle paths. The land was planted to cotton and the fields required for their working some two hundred Negroes. The health of all these hands, in addition of course to the management of the household servants, was Mrs. McCord's care. She established a nursery where the women left their babies when they went to work in the fields and a hospital with attendants whom she trained and supervised. Every morning she rode down for an inspection of the quarters and her pony stood always ready saddled in case of· an emergency. She was as prompt to set out at midnight as at noon. An expert and fearless rider, she had one of those legendary horses no one else can manage, a little Canadian mustang called Pixie whose exploits made favorite family stories.

Mrs. McCord took her duties very seriously. Asked once why she wore so little jewelry, she replied (thinking, surely, of her prototype Cornelia) that a woman with two hundred children could not afford diamonds. Her efficiency and resourcefulness were a byword among her friends, and her own domain made such constant demand upon her for wisdom, mercy, and kindness that she was not conscious of the narrower life of her less wealthy neighbors. That an intelligent woman might find herself without proper scope for her abilities seemed to the mistress of Lang Syne simply preposterous. Insular, like so many Southerners, for all her education and travel, Louisa McCord had for her activity no standard of comparison beyond the admiring exclamations of such idle intelligent women as Mrs. Chesnut (of the *Diary from Dixie*). She never heard, of course, comments like those which James B. Angell, who was most hospitably entertained at Lang Syne, set down in his diary, and published, sixty years later, in his *Reminiscences*.

That observant young Yankee, who was to become president of the University of Michigan, took, for his health, a horseback trip through the South shortly after his graduation from Brown in 1849. He and his companion had letters to the McCords who gave them their first taste of plantation living. This corrected, he wrote, "our impression that the life of the planter and his wife was one free from care. They did have more leisure than the northern farmer. But careful management was required to secure good profits." That phrase about the farmer would have astonished Mrs. McCord who was convinced that her daily schedule was far more arduous than that of any Northern housewife.

Angell was impressed by the organization at Lang Syne, everything "very systematical," and he found the master's relationship with his Negroes paternal and kind. When he watched a slave auction in Georgia and saw a traveler at an inn cruelly beating his black boy with a leathern thong, he wrote that he was now witnessing a side of slavery "that we had learned nothing of in the hospitable homes of South Carolina." Yet he set down a little incident about one of those hospitable homes which, occurring just as he was leaving Lang Syne, made a deep impression upon him.

The Negro driver who took them to the railway station was "a grave elderly man, a Baptist preacher, in fact, for his people."

I ventured to say to him, "You servants must all be very happy in your lot with such a kind master and mistress." He answered not a word, but looked at me with a surprised and pathetic air, which seemed to me to say, "You, who are from the North, ought to know that slavery is not a happy condition." I dropped the conversation, but I have never forgotten the expression of his countenance.

In the year of the Bastiat translation David McCord, who was genuinely interested in encouraging his wife's literary activity, secretly made up a collection of her poems and had them printed by Cary and Hart in Philadelphia. The surprise aroused not her pleasure but her anger. The verses she thought, quite rightly, were not ready for publication, and her Roman response to her husband's gift was an energetic attempt to buy up and suppress the whole edition. Copies of *My Dreams* are hard to come by though the most finished of the poems, "The Voice of Years," appears in many of the Southern anthologies.

The poem on which Louisa McCord wished her reputation to rest is *Caius Gracchus*, a verse tragedy in five acts, which she published in 1851. This was literary pioneering. A good many Southern ladies indited verses but, as *De Bow's* said in reviewing *Caius Gracchus*, most female poets write exactly alike; there is no distinguishing one from the other; the only poetesses of the South who command attention are Mrs. Gilman of Charleston and Mrs. McCord. Very few women, certainly, attempted any such sustained effort as a drama. "A tragedy by a Southron, and a lady," said the *Southern Quarterly*, "is surely no such ordinary event, that we should pass it with indifference," and *De Bow's* called the author a "brilliant anomaly."

Most of the critics spoke of *Caius Gracchus* as closet drama, not intended for the stage, a polite way of saying that it is not very exciting. Some of them thought the verse insufficiently polished, but all agreed that it was powerful and full of fine thoughts.

Those fine thoughts and its autobiographic qualities are what make the tragedy interesting today. Southern statesmen were so accustomed to thinking of themselves as neo-Romans that no great effort of imagination on the dramatist's part was required to make Cornelia an idealized portrait of herself and Caius Gracchus a combination of her father in his youth and her son as she hoped he would be in manhood. She makes no attempt to force parallels between the Roman and the contemporary political situation but all the characters speak the word "Senator" with such bitterness that one inevitably hears beside it the adjective "Yankee." Caius is presented as the champion of the people against the despotic and greedy patricians. He is proud of the fact that his father was plebian:

> Oh! learn ye that there is no higher place
> Than that from which the self-ennobled, turns
> A helping hand to lend to who would rise
> Like him from abjectness.

Caius' eloquence as an orator is described in the kind of terms that were used about Langdon Cheves. He has skill, too, as a negotiator with foreign powers and as a colonial organizer. But his chief role is that of defender of the people against the encroachments of the Senate who are appropriating to themselves public lands and supplies that should go into the common garner.

The wife of Caius, Licinia, is presented as sweet and loving but young and uninformed about affairs of state. She does not look beyond the personal situation and is careful only for her husband's safety and comfort. It is his mother, Cornelia, who spurs him to public action, gives him wise political advice, and attempts, though unsuccessfully, that is the tragedy, to curb his youthful ambition.

. . . you have let
Your passion much mislead you.

.　　.　　.　　.　　.　　.　　.　　.　　.

The time's unripe, and you would force it on,
Not by a gentle teaching to the truth,
But gag it to your own ideas of right,
And force mankind to gulp your system down.

Cornelia speaks also Louisa McCord's interpretation of woman's role as propagandist:

I reverence human mind
And with a mingled love and pride I kneel
To nature's inborn majesty in man.
But as I reverence therefore would I lend
My feeble aid, this mighty power to lead
To its true aim and end.

To lead nature's inborn majesty Louisa McCord continued to bend her best efforts, writing fiery paragraphs in defense of the Southern cause and especially of the misunderstood institution of Negro slavery. As ardently as Maria Child she felt the compulsion to open America's eyes to the true facts. Surely the abolitionist would not continue on his headlong course if he could really see where it was leading. It was the duty of those who knew to place the facts where they could not be evaded. Some Southern ladies, like Mrs. Eastman, Caroline Hentz, and Caroline Rush, were writing novels that showed slavery as a benevolent institution but that a female should attempt to set forth such views in learned articles was a phenomenon, and not only in the South. New England and the Middle States had their female journalists who dashed off pungent paragraphs on questions of the day but their number was small and they seldom extended their thinking beyond the limits of a newspaper column. Louisa Mc-Cord's elaborate reasoned presentations of social and political ideas were certainly as strong-minded productions as the century had seen, though their content was thoroughly conservative. Mrs. Sarah Josepha Hale, who, as editor of the *Lady's Book* and compiler of a biographical dictionary of eminent women, knew all there was to know about contemporary feminine attainment, said that Louisa McCord "has distinguished herself in what may be styled political literature, a species of writing seldom attempted by woman." "The warm enthusiasm of her nature," Mrs. Hale goes on, "was intensified by her Southern patriotism, and these feelings have caused her to enter earnestly into questions of State policy, and lend her ready pen to uphold what to her seemed the most important truths. . . . we think her Essays will be found, upon fair comparison, equal to any that form the higher articles in the very best Reviews."

Mrs. Hale did not exaggerate. Mrs. McCord's arguments proceed logically from premises which were to her axiomatic. She begs a question, when necessary, with legal skill. She has a keen eye for the soft places in her adversary's case; her wit is "temperately bright," as Mrs. Hale says a woman's should be; and, though her irony is often heavy-handed, it is never dull; she carries the reader along in her own passionate excited concern. In able articles for *De Bow's*, the *Southern Literary Messenger*, and the *Southern Quarterly Review* she stated the case for slavery as the best minds of the South liked to put it: slavery is the way of life the Creator has ordained for the black race.

Science, the argument runs, has made it clear (Agassiz,

because he speaks from abolitionist Cambridge, is in this connection a name to conjure with) that whatever their origin, the races of mankind are, and have been for eons, fundamentally distinct, with intellectual and spiritual capacities as different as their physical color and structure. Give him what opportunity you may, the Negro will never equal the achievement of the white. Isolated, he exists in contented barbarism; in contact with a stronger race he must either disappear—see for instance how the free black population is shrinking in the North—or come under the rule and tutelage of the white. A combination of the races is essential to the progress of the world, for only the black, with his special physical adaptation, can cultivate the land in those climates where important staples (cotton of course in particular) can be grown. And the black man can work only under white care and guidance. Slavery, therefore, is a noble human cooperation with the divine plan. That the system is sometimes abused, that it is, like every human institution, imperfect, is no indication that the plan is wrong, merely that mankind is fallible. In the Southern American states slavery has attained its highest perfection in recorded history. The institution is daily improving as the world moves in its upward path of progress. All we have now to fear is the wanton meddling of ignorant utopians who fancy they can improve upon the divine scheme.

This argument Louisa McCord presented with admirable variety seven different times. In April, 1851, she discussed for the *Southern Quarterly Review* a handful of scientific pamphlets on the "Diversity of Races," making particular play with Professor Agassiz's remarks on the "Diversity of the Origin of Human Species." A few months later she turned a review of Kingsley's *Alton Locke* into an article on "Negro and White Slavery." In 1852 she reviewed for *De Bow's*, *Negro-Mania* by John Campbell, "an examination of the falsely assumed equality of the races of men." In 1853 she reviewed *Uncle Tom's Cabin* for the *Southern Quarterly*, discussed for *De Bow's* "British Philanthropy and American Slavery," and for the *Southern Literary Messenger* made another attack on English self-righteousness, "Charity Which Does Not Begin at Home," using as a point of departure articles in *Blackwood's* and the *Westminster*. In 1854 she reviewed for the *Southern Quarterly* "Carey on the Slave Trade," and how it may be extinguished, a prejudiced and ignorant work, useful only because it exposes to view the "mischievous tripartite power" which menaces our republic: protection, communism, abolition.

The audience to whom Louisa McCord addresses her remarks in all these articles is twofold, the Northern and the English abolitionists. She labors, though it seems to her often a labor of Sisyphus, to make them understand the true nature of slavery. She rebukes them, too, the English in particular, for their concern with their neighbors' sins when their own are crying out so loudly for reform. Charles Kingsley's pictures of industrial misery in London furnished particularly good grist for her argument. She had of course, as her father's daughter, no love for the English, and their readiness to accept Yankee abolitionist accounts of conditions in the South stirred her to peculiar wrath. When she came to review *Uncle Tom's Cabin* she included in her discussion a laudatory comment from the *Westminster Review* and addressed herself primarily to the deluded English reader who was swallowing as truth the "loathsome rakings" of Mrs. Stowe's "foul fancy."

William Gilmore Simms, thinking it a sort of poetic justice to match woman against woman, asked Mrs. Mc-Cord to engage Mrs. Stowe in the pages of the *Southern Quarterly* and she agreed to the combat. Her strategy was carefully planned. The important thing was to show the people in England, and in Europe, and in our Northern states, who were buying the book by the hundred thousands, that Mrs. Stowe's pictures of Southern life have no basis in fact, that they are simply the creations of a "Monk Lewis" imagination pandering to the popular demand for horrors. This she proceeds to demonstrate:

Mrs. Stowe's ignorance of her subject is apparent as soon as one opens the book. The very first scene, which sets the story in motion, the scene where the planter Shelby is forced by debt to sell his valued servant Uncle Tom, is preposterous. Who ever heard of a Southern gentleman admitting a slave trader to his house, sitting down with him to discuss business over a glass of wine? And what is this curious debt which so weighs upon Mr. Shelby? If it can be settled by the sale of one Negro it cannot amount to more than $1,000. Has Mr. Shelby no friends? Will no bank trust him? Why must he sell to a brutal dealer the faithful Tom and a baby, torn from its mother's arms? It is apparent that Mrs. Stowe knows little of plantation life and the institution of which she purports to be writing.

Even the speech of her dramatis personae is uncharacteristic and absurd. The elegant Augustine St. Clare of New Orleans says: "Isn't it dreadful tiresome?" "I've travelled in England some." "That isn't my affair *as* I know of," and employs other quaint turns of phrase heard only in New England. The other Southern ladies and gentlemen carry on in the same vein and while they speak this vulgar Yankee English, the Louisiana Negroes talk pure Kentuck.

Nor are their manners any better than their vocabulary. St. Clare's languorous wife calls her maid a "good for nothing nigger" and is enraged at the suggestion that Mammy, who has been separated from her husband and children, can really miss them, can love "her little dirty babies as I love Eva."

Never, we contend, was there the Southern woman, brought up in decent associations, at once so heartless and so foolish, that, supposing it possible for her to feel nothing in such a case, would not, for mere fashion and gentility sake, imitate those feelings of which she would know it to be her shame to be devoid. It is not the *fashion* with us to hang out the flag of hard-heartedness. If "*the system*" necessitates in us that short-coming from virtue, (as the omniscient Mrs. Stowe most dogmatically asserts that it does, has done, must and ever will do,) at least we have learned the hypocrisy to conceal the calamitous deficiency under which we labour.

And when Mrs. St. Clare continues, "I keep my cowhide about, and sometimes I do lay it on (!!!)" "we did break out into most uncontrollable laughter."

To her ignorance and inaccuracy Mrs. Stowe adds illogic. If the slave is a chattel for which he has paid, why should the owner destroy his property, whipping him to death, when he could obtain a large equivalent of his outlay simply by transferring him to other hands? Again, if the slave is in the master's eyes a mere animal, a piece of property, why does she suppose any feeling of rivalry in the master's breast, any impulsion to humiliate the slave?

It is perfectly clear that Mrs. Stowe has never set foot in a slave state, or, if she has, it has been nothing more than a crossing of the Kentucky border. (This guess so precisely corresponds to the fact that it is impressive. Mrs. Stowe's experience of Southern life was a visit of a few weeks in Washington, Kentucky, made when she was twenty-two. She was undoubtedly entertained on some of the neighboring plantations but she stayed in a comfortable middle-class house in the village.)

In a border state, constantly open to the attacks of meddling fanaticism, every man feels that his property (while the legal institutions of his state, formed for its protection, are staggering) stands but by a very doubtful tenure, and he naturally looks forward to parting with it some way or other. . . . By this habit of mind, a severance of old ties and affection soon springs up. The child is no longer educated to think that the slave is almost a part of himself, a dependent to live and die with. The idea is constantly held forward of some necessary change; and how to make that change, at the least loss to himself, will of course, be a frequent question with the property holder. Then comes the clash between interest and humanity, and the old link of mutual affection broken, too often the sick and weak negro becomes a burden, the strong one simply a property. *This* is no longer the slavery we love to defend. This bastard growth of abolitionism grafted on selfishness, is *not* Southern United States Slavery. It is border state slavery, from which, thanks to abolitionism, have sprung *some* (thank God! only *some*, only a few) of those horrors which abolition writers delight to depict.

In addition to her very limited personal experience Mrs. Stowe offers in support of her testimony on slavery only vague statements and impressions of friends, and of a brother traveling to New Orleans. From his letter she derived the character of Legree, whose fist was "calloused with knocking down niggers." This brother is not a very impressive authority. "Who has not seen the green Yankee youth opening his eyes and mouth for every piece of stray intelligence; eager for horrors; gulping the wildest tales, and exaggerating even as he swallows them?"

To conclude. We have undertaken the defence of slavery in no temporizing vein. We do *not* say it is a necessary evil. We do *not* allow that it is a temporary make-shift to choke the course of Providence for man's convenience. It is *not* "a sorrow and a wrong to be lived down." We proclaim it, on the contrary, a Godlike dispensation, a providential caring for the weak, and a refuge for the portionless. Nature's outcast, as for centuries he appeared to be, he—even from the dawning of tradition, the homeless, houseless, useless negro—suddenly assumes a place, suddenly becomes one of the great levers of civilization. . . . Christian slavery, in its full development, free from the fretting annoyance and galling bitterness of abolition interference, is the brightest sunbeam which Omniscience has destined for his [the Negro's] existence.

The list of articles by L.S.M. has no entries in 1855. In that year David McCord died and his wife, deprived of his enthusiastic encouragement and burdened with new responsibilities, suffering too from ill-health and eyestrain, found no energy to spare for propagandizing the Southern cause. The most important thing in life now seemed to her the education of her son. To facilitate that the family spent the greater part of the year in Columbia, living in a house which David McCord had built just across the road from the campus of South Carolina College (now the University of South Carolina). Judge Cheves spent his last years there with his daughter.

After her father's death in 1857 Louisa McCord, weary in body and spirit, sailed to Europe for that change of scene which was the great nineteenth-century specific for all ills. She carried appropriate letters to literary people who received her as a literary lady and the remedy worked. In 1859 she was back in Columbia steeled to carry on the education of her children, to direct the plantation on which their livelihood depended, and to perform, during the years of war, a service for which South Carolina counts her among the state's heroines.

The liveliest pictures of Louisa McCord which any of her contemporaries have left us were drawn in the war years in the diary of Mary Boykin Chesnut. Mrs. Chesnut —her husband was aid to Jefferson Davis and a brigadier general in the Confederate Army—made, and kept, the resolution to set down a daily account of her personal life during the war. Such a record, she thought, might be valuable to posterity. She spent many months in Columbia where Mrs. McCord was an even more dominant figure than she had been in peacetime. In 1862, when civilians still had carriage horses, she and Mrs. McCord drove out together every day.

June 4, 1862:—Mrs. Preston and I speak in whispers, but Mrs. McCord scorns whispers, and speaks out. She says: "There are our soldiers. Since the world began there never were better, but God does not deign to send us a general worthy of them. I do not mean drill-sergeants or military old maids, who will not fight until everything is just so. The real ammunition of our war is faith in ourselves and enthusiasm in our cause. West Point sits down on enthusiasm, laughs it to scorn. It wants discipline. And now comes a new danger, these blockade runners. They are filling their pockets and they gibe and sneer at the fools who fight. Don't you see this Stonewall, how he fires the soldiers' hearts; he will be our leader, maybe after all. They say he does not care how many are killed. His business is to save the country, not the army. He fights to win, God bless him, and he wins. If they do not want to be killed, they can stay home. They say he leaves the sick and wounded to be cared for by those whose business it is to do so. His business is war. They say he wants to hoist the black flag, have a short, sharp, decisive war and end it. He is a Christian soldier.

Early that spring Mrs. McCord had raised and equipped a company for her son, then twenty-one and lately married. The Ladies Clothing Association, of which she was president, made the uniforms from material which she provided, regulation grey cloth stitched with silk. The men looked, the ladies proudly recorded, a company of young patricians.

Foreseeing, as not all Southern women did, that the struggle would be long, Mrs. McCord began at once to plant provision crops at Lang Syne. The country, she believed, should be made self-supporting. She set up, too, a variety of workshops and trained her "people" to skills in weaving cloth and making shoes which had not been practiced on the plantations for fifty years. Everything on the place was laid under contribution to the army. The lead pipes of an elaborate system of waterworks went to be melted into bullets; carpets were cut up into blankets; the contents of wool mattresses was spun into yarn for soldiers' socks, and Louisa McCord's energetic mind invented original devices of conservation. She made her Negroes save the hair of all the rabbits they killed and devised a method of mixing it with ravelings of black silk and spinning it into yarn which could be knitted up as officers' gloves.

Her most important work was done for the hospital established in the buildings of South Carolina College. Her house became a depot where neighbors sent in whatever they could spare from their meager larders. There were vegetables, scraps of meat, even the refuse parts of beeves killed for market. Every morning Mrs. McCord looked over the strange assortment and put whatever was wholesome into a great pot, seasoning the stew herself to make it as palatable as possible. Big pans of cornbread were made and plates of the food were set out on a long dresser on the back piazza for those of the sick and wounded who could drag themselves across the street to get a meal. Fifty to a hundred men came daily.

To those who could not leave their beds Mrs. McCord carried such delicacies as she could gather, and all day long she went about the wards, writing letters, relieving pain, comforting the dying. She could never see work that needed doing without doing it or things going crooked without trying to set them straight and before long she was a sort of unofficial superintendent of the whole hospital. "I remember once saying to my husband," writes the wife of the chief surgeon St. Julien Ravenel, " 'St. Julien, two ladies were here today, who said they wondered at your letting Mrs. McCord manage your Hospital.' He answered abruptly, 'The more she manages the better, every bit of her that isn't enthusiasm is common sense.' "

Among other duties Mrs. McCord undertook the direction of the volunteer nurses, arranging their schedules and trying to teach them how to make themselves really useful. Like Mrs. Swisshelm she had a fine contempt for the woman who came to the hospital dressed for the role of ministering angel instead of for the dirty bloody tasks of army nursing, and, like Mrs. Swisshelm, she had no hesitation in saying so. When, she told Mrs. Chesnut, she saw women coming in angel sleeves, displaying their white arms, and in muslin, showing their beautiful shoulders, she felt disposed to order them off the premises. She added an angry account of a "lovely lady nurse" who asked a rough old soldier what she could do for him and was answered roundly, "Kiss me!" Mrs. McCord's fury, Mrs. Chesnut records, was not at the incident but "at the woman's telling it," because it brought her hospital into disrepute.

And while she directed and scolded and comforted, her eye everywhere, Louisa McCord's hands were perpetually busy with her knitting needles. All Southern ladies of course knitted for the soldiers but Mrs. McCord's knitting was legendary. Three pairs of socks a day was the stint she set herself and accomplished month after long month. "The click of her needles could be heard," wrote one of her friends, "above the sound of her weeping." For Louisa McCord had not only South Carolina's sorrows to bear but anxiety and grief of her own. Cheves McCord, her able, promising only son, the Caius Gracchus of her drama, the center of her work and hope, was wounded at the battle of Second Manassas. He was thought to be recovering, was permitted to make a brief visit home, then, suddenly, died, in Richmond, from an inflammation of the brain excited by what had been supposed the slightest of his three wounds.

"Spent today with Mrs. McCord at her hospital," wrote Mrs. Chesnut on August 2, 1864. "She is dedicating her grief for her son, sanctifying it, one might say, by giving up her soul and body, her days and nights, to the wounded soldiers at her hospital. Every moment of her time is surrendered to their needs."

Of the approach of Sherman's troops Mrs. McCord had warning through General Chesnut's letters to his wife but she decided not to flee with her friend but to stay by her hospital and her home. In the accounts of the terrible night when the city burned—she believed of course that the fire was set—there are references to her as a tower of strength among frightened women. Her own house, which General Howard used as headquarters during the occupation, escaped the flames.

The dark days after Lee's surrender were lightened a little by the marriage of her younger daughter. Mrs. Chesnut has a note, written at Camden, on Mrs. McCord's determined attempt to celebrate the occasion properly.

June 12, 1865—A wedding to be. Lou McCord's. And Mrs. McCord is going about frantically, looking for eggs "to mix and make into wedding-cake," and finding none. She now drives the funniest little one-mule vehicle.

Danger and privation Louisa McCord could cope with but not submission, She was so reluctant to take the oath of allegiance to the Federal Government that she spent the next two years in Canada. The desire to dispose of her own property finally constrained her to go through the hated formality and she settled in the home of her daughter, Mrs. Augustine T. Smythe, in Charleston.

Twelve years she lived there—her death took place on November 23, 1879—coming into public notice only occasionally as sponsor of some Confederate memorial, never reconciled to the loss of the lost cause, sure always that in using her pen in its behalf she had followed the divine directive.

> It is a glorious right to rouse the soul,
> The reasoning heart that in a nation sleeps!
> And Wisdom is a lagard at her task
> When but in closet speculation toiling
> She doth forget to share her thought abroad
> And make mankind her heir.

South Carolina College when Mrs. McCord lived across the road

L. Maria Child in 1850 and in 1865

Dusting Mirrors

L. MARIA CHILD

"Too much cannot be said on the importance of giving children early habits of observation." When, in 1832, Maria Child wrote that dictum in her *Mother's Book* she was anxious not only that the young should be made to see truth but that they should be helped to enjoy the world. And she was making, really, an autobiographical statement. Observation was for her the first of the virtues. The greater part of her long and active life was spent in teaching people to see, to see often things they did not want to look at. "I sweep dead leaves out of paths and dust mirrors," she said once in describing her daily activities and she might as well have been describing her method of propaganda: she set out her facts always so clear and clean that it was impossible not to see them. To thousands of men and women, including distinguished abolitionists like Charles Sumner, Thomas Wentworth Higginson, and William Ellery Channing, her books first made clear the true nature of slavery.

Lydia Maria Francis (the family called her Maria) began her own observation of the world on September 11, 1802, in Medford, Massachusetts. Of her mother it is recorded only that she had "a spirit busy in doing good," a spirit which her daughter inherited. Her father was a baker, the originator of the "Medford Cracker," so excellent a cracker, the story runs, that orders came to him from Europe, even from Russia. He was, like the Beechers' blacksmith grandfather, an artisan who loved to read and who believed in education for his children. His eldest son, Convers, six years older than Maria, became a Unitarian clergyman and Parkman Professor in the Harvard Divinity School.

It was Convers who supervised his sister's studies, directed her reading, and tried to answer her curious questions. "Do not forget," concludes a letter written when she was seventeen, "that I asked you about the 'flaming cherubims,' the effects of distance horizontal or perpendicular, 'Orlando Furioso,' and Lord Byron." Maria told her brother that he had formed her mind but certainly he never managed to impart to it any of the caution for which he was notorious. That caution often exasperated to anger his distinguished disciple Theodore Parker who had more in common temperamentally with his mentor's sister. Maria thought Parker "the greatest man, morally and intellectually, that our country ever produced."

Maria Francis was visiting her brother, pastor at the time of the Unitarian Church in Watertown, Massachusetts, when, at the age of twenty-one, she discovered her literary vocation. The story, repeated again and again by contemporary biographers, was first set down by that indefatigable anthologist Rufus Griswold who probably had it from Maria herself.

Waiting for her brother in his study one day in the summer of 1823 Maria Francis happened to pick up an old copy of the *North American Review* (April, 1821) and was attracted by an article on a long narrative poem called *Yamoyden*.

We are gratified [wrote the Rev. J. G. Palfrey] with the appearance of Yamoyden, for a reason distinct from that of being an accession to the amount of good poetry. We are glad that somebody has at last found out the unequalled fitness of our early history for the purposes of a work of fiction. For ourselves, we know not the country or age which has such capacities in this view as N. England in its early day; nor do we suppose it easy to imagine any element of the sublime, the wonderful, the picturesque and the pathetic, which is not to be found here by him who shall hold the witch-hazel wand that can trace it.

That witch-hazel wand Maria Francis felt suddenly in her grasp. It pointed her to her first mission: a novel she saw might be a work of patriotism. She took up a pen from her brother's table and began to write.

It was then about noon. Convers Francis returned a little before afternoon service and his sister asked him to look at the first chapter of a novel, set in Naumkeak (Salem) in 1629. When he looked up from the manuscript and explained, "But, Maria, did you *really* write this? Do you mean what you say, that it is entirely your own?" Maria Francis' fate was set; she became a literary lady. In six weeks she had finished *Hobomok*, and Cummings, Hilliard and Company of Boston agreed to print it. Mindful of her patriotic mission she signed it "By an American."

The most interesting thing about *Hobomok* is not its setting but its study of the motives which drive the lovely heroine to become the bride of an Indian warrior. The situation may quite possibly have been suggested by

Yamoyden where a well-born young lady is united with a noble savage, but Miss Francis is concerned with something more than a striking plot. She shows her Mary Conant nearly mad with despair at the news that her lover has been lost at sea. The poor girl can find no comfort in her home for her gentle mother has lately died and her stern, old father was largely responsible for the lover's exile from the colony. Even Mary's religion merely intensifies her despair; the Puritanism of Naumkeak has stupefied her mind with "an ill directed belief in the decrees of heaven and the utter fruitlessness of all human endeavor." She turns to Hobomok, the one person in Salem who has shown her unvarying kindness and admiration.

What follows is somewhat less realistic. Mary, Hobomok, and his old mother live a quiet life together in a tastefully decorated wigwam; Mary bears a child; and finally, when the lost lover, who was not drowned, returns, the noble Hobomok goes through the Indian form of divorce and vanishes forever into the wilderness.

This curious plot shocked both reading public and critics. "It is in very bad taste, to say the least," wrote Jared Sparks in the *North American*, but he admired the book's other qualities and Boston as a whole agreed with him. There was enthusiastic approval of the animated descriptions of scenes and persons, the agreeable style, and the picture of the times. Female literary success was then so rare as to be exciting. Everybody talked about *Hobomok* and the Boston Athenæum bestowed on Miss Francis an almost unique honor, a free ticket of admission to its library. Of course she went to work at once on another novel. In 1825 "the author of *Hobomok*" published *The Rebels: Or, Boston before the Revolution*.

The Rebels is not quite so exciting as its title promises. It is heavily charged with patriotic sentiment and political conversation but it is better organized than its predecessor and decidedly better as a picture of a period. Prerevolutionary Boston did not present such dangerous blanks to the romantic fancy as the shadowier era of the Puritan and the noble redman. The talk is stilted enough but it was based on sound models. The speech against the Stamp Act which the young authoress invented for James Otis was quoted in schoolbooks as an example of that patriot's oratory.

The public liked *The Rebels* and the *North American* predicted that, "notwithstanding its many defects," it would take "a high rank in the estimation of all admirers of descriptive and pathetic eloquence." Miss Francis found herself a local celebrity. Adulation did her no harm, for she had a head not easily turned and literature was her proper calling. In fact one cannot help wondering whether, born in the twentieth century, she might not have made a really good novelist. A little of the scientific psychology she would have picked up in any good college to direct her accurate intuitions, a little instruction in historical method to channel her enthusiastic curiosity, and she might have disciplined her sentimental sympathy and undocumented imagination into a vigorous and effective realism.

In any case Maria Francis had found the work she wanted to do. It was, though, work more delightful than remunerative so she resorted to the conventional expedient of opening a small school in Watertown and, a year later, the unconventional expedient of editing a magazine for the young, one of the earliest in the country. *The*

Juvenile Miscellany was, wrote Margaret Fuller, "much and deservedly esteemed by children."

It was during these years in Watertown that Maria Francis began her lifelong friendship with Margaret Fuller. That brilliant and ambitious girl, eight years Maria's junior, was delighted to discover a companion who shared her enthusiasm for learning and whose thinking was quite free from cant and pretense. Miss Francis' conversation, she wrote, "is charming,—she brings all her powers to bear upon it; her style is varied, and she has a very pleasant and spirited way of thinking." They read Locke together as introduction to a course of English metaphysics and then Mme. de Staël on Locke. Margaret decided to take the brilliant Frenchwoman as a model instead of "the useful Edgeworth," and Maria made her the subject of the first biography in the Ladies Family Library which she began to edit a few years later.

It was in Watertown, too, that Maria Francis made the acquaintance of David Lee Child who was studying law there with his uncle. After one of their first evenings together she made an entry in her journal: "He is the most gallant man that has lived since the sixteenth century and needs nothing but helmet, shield, and chain armor to make him a complete knight of chivalry."

That, from the little we know of him, was an accurate estimate of David Child. He had not only charm and courage but that inner compulsion to defend the oppressed which one associates with the Round Table. And the helmet covered an excellent brain. These were all qualities to attract Maria Francis. She had them herself, tempered with a practicality which David Child lacked. In 1820 he had left his post of secretary of legation at Lisbon to fight in Spain against the French because, he said, he felt it his duty to defend liberty. Now he was devoting more and more of his energies to the unremunerative, unpopular cause of the American slave.

The Francis-Child friendship seems to have been a Benedict and Beatrice affair with much witty pretense of antagonism on either side to hide an affection rapidly growing warm. The courtship went on for three years until, admitted to the bar, David Child felt justified in asking Maria Francis to be his wife. George Ticknor Curtis, who as a small boy watched a good many of their meetings over the bannisters in his mother's house, tells the story of the proposal which, he says, lasted four hours and a half. Mrs. Curtis, who had discreetly retired to the second floor, waited patiently for the raising of the siege but David Child's horse, tethered close to the front porch, found the time too long and pawed the piazza steps so vigorously that his master had to dash out at intervals to quiet him.

The marriage took place on October 19, 1828, and the couple set up housekeeping in Boston. It was a very happy though a highly unconventional ménage: the wife thought for herself and she earned the major portion of the family income. Maria Child believed in freedom for the slave but she did not share her husband's abolition principles. She respected them, though, and was ready, as always, to listen and to learn. She was ready, too, to accept the consequences of his putting his legal skill at the disposition of fugitive slaves and oppressed Negroes, a ruinous practice of course for a young lawyer. Mrs. Child undertook to do the domestic labor of the household—an economy which caused remark—and she kept their expenses to a minimum. Curtis thought it worth reporting that when they entertained him at dinner they served a savory meat pie, roasted potatoes, and baked Indian pudding, no dessert, no wine, no beverage; but it was, apparently, a very good meat pie.

Her experience in domestic economy Maria Child converted promptly into literary capital. *The Frugal Housewife*, which she published in 1829, went into forty editions, gratefully purchased by "the poor" for whom she said it was written. It did not escape, though, the satiric comment of N. P. Willis who made great play with one of her economical dicta: "Hard gingerbread is nice" (it keeps so well). Maria Francis, unlike most literary young ladies, had not surrendered to Willis' charm and had declined to write for his *Mirror*.

Next, drawing on her experience as a teacher and editor of the *Juvenile Miscellany*, though she had no children of her own, Mrs. Child published a wise and charming *Mother's Book*, which went into English and German as well as many American editions. Then *The Girls' Own Book* with rules for games, directions for making baskets and "ornaments," and instruction in sewing and gardening. For girls also was *The First Settlers of New England* as Related by a Mother to Her Children, an attempt to prove by history what *Hobomok* had demonstrated by romance: that the Indian is a noble creature, hostile and barbarous only when the white man provokes him with cruelty and deceit. Like Jane Swisshelm and Grace Greenwood, Maria Child found the red man "repugnant" but she felt that he must have justice and that it was her duty to help him to it.

In 1832 Maria Child began the editing of the Ladies Family Library, a series designed to "suit the taste, and interest the feelings of women." Each volume, the prospectus states, will be prepared by the editor and will contain more or less original writing—in those happy days before copyright there were no limits on the length of a compiler's quotations. Maria Child was skillful at compiling and condensing and she managed to infuse into anything she composed the pleasant freshness of her own interest in the subject. She was a popularizer of the best kind, simplifying without condescension.

I have been told [she wrote in one of her prefaces] that I did not moralize enough, or explain my own opinions with sufficient fulness. To this I can only answer, that I am describing the minds of others, not my own. It seems to me that the beauty of biography consists in simplicity, clearness, and brevity. I wish to give faithful portraits of individuals, and leave my readers in freedom to analyze their expression.

For the first volume she chose Mme. de Staël, whom she and Margaret Fuller had admired for her brilliant mind and her readiness to labor in the public service, and another revolutionary heroine, Mme. Roland. The second volume treats Mme. de Guyon and Lady Russell. The third contains some two score brief biographies of *Good Wives* ranging from "Calphurnia, wife of Pliny" to "Mrs. LaFayette." This was followed by a *History of the Condition of Women in All Ages*, not, the editor explains, an essay on woman's rights, nor yet a philosophical investigation of the relation of the sexes, simply a collection of facts presented with the idea that they will excite thought and provide material for argument. This, from the beginning to the end, was Maria Child's method of propaganda: to dust the mirror so that her readers could not choose but see.

Everything she wrote in any vein pleased both public and critics and her reputation grew. "We are not sure," said the *North American*, "that any woman in our country would outrank Mrs. Child. . . . Few female writers, if any, have done more or better things for our literature, in its lighter or graver departments." This was a pleasant position to occupy and pleasant, too, were the literary friendships her work brought her in Boston and Cambridge. It was not an easy life but it had come to be a very good one, and full of promise for the future, when, quite deliberately, she pulled it all down about her head.

In 1833 Maria Child published *An Appeal in Behalf of that Class of Americans Called Africans*. The curious title alone was frightening to her contemporaries and the whole book seemed to respectable Boston dangerously incendiary. Her friends, all but a very few, and her large national circle of readers and admirers drew away in alarm. Women who had been proud to bow to the distinguished Mrs. Child now cut her on Mt. Auburn Street. The Athenæum, scandalized that its shelves had been utilized for the production of such a fanatical document, wrote in haste withdrawing the privileges it had bestowed. The sale of her books declined sharply and subscriptions to the *Juvenile Miscellany* were canceled so rapidly that it soon became futile to publish the little magazine at all.

Outwardly the *Appeal* is a quiet document. There is no invective, no denunciation, simply information set down almost without comment. It begins with a history of slavery, describing its true nature in the United States, and then considers the effect of the institution upon the Negro and upon his owner. All the assertions are docu-

mented with chapter and verse, with citations of laws and
legal testimony, with corroborative little stories horrifying in their objectivity. Then remedies are considered.
The inadequacy of colonization and the frequent evil
motives behind the plan are made clear and the contrasting
purpose of the Anti-Slavery Society is explained. The
propaganda method is simple but it is deadly; Boston was
quite right to be alarmed. The *Appeal* became a power-
fully influential document. More than one dangerous
abolitionist ascribed his conversion to the cause to his reading of Mrs. Child. William Ellery Channing, who had
never met her before, walked out from Boston to Rox-
bury to tell her she had convinced him that slavery was a
subject on which he should no longer remain silent; John
Palfrey said to her years later that it was the *Appeal* which
caused him to liberate his slaves; and Charles Sumner
wrote that it had an important effect upon his course in
Congress.

Maria Child's own conversion was a surprise not only
to respectable Boston but to the abolitionists themselves.
They were accustomed to see her at their meetings but
they supposed that she came merely out of courtesy to
her husband; they had never thought of her as a potential
fighter in their ranks. It was David Child who changed
her point of view by spreading out pertinent documents
for her observation. There are telling sentences in her
anti-slavery books which mark the progress of her conviction, the particular facts which she found inescapable.

I have read not a few Reports of Cases in Southern Courts;
and those reports did more than any thing else to make me
an abolitionist.

These assertions [that abolition would cause servile insurrections] have been so often, and so dogmatically repeated, that many truly kind-hearted people have believed there was some truth in them. I myself, (may God forgive me for it!) have often, in thoughtless ignorance, made the same remarks. An impartial and careful examination has led me to the conviction that slavery causes insurrections, while emancipation prevents them.

I once had a very strong prejudice against anti-slavery;— (I am ashamed to think *how* strong—for mere prejudice should never be stubborn,) but a candid examination has convinced me, that I was in an error. I made the common mistake of taking things for granted, without stopping to investigate.

Though not the first, Maria Child was one of the earliest of the courageous little band of men and women who fought the good fight through that period which Harriet Martineau called the Martyr Age in the United States. The adjective is accurate; both spiritual and physical courage were required of the abolitionists, and Maria Child had both. Once committed to the cause, she battled for it with all her might. The Lord, she said, had more than enough waiters; fighters were what he needed in his service now. As a Boston abolitionist she learned what it meant to face a mob and she used to tell, with a certain amusement, pacifist as she was, of the time when, at a meeting in the Music Hall, she collared a man who was shaking his fist in Wendell Phillips' face, and of her surprise when he tumbled down. Someone cried out to her, "This is no place for women," and she retorted promptly, "They are needed here to teach civilization to men." In 1839 she was writing to Lucretia Mott: "A little while ago I rejoiced that I was growing more entirely and universally tolerant. Now, I cannot abide the proud, self-sufficient word. What right have I, or any other fallible mortal, to be *tolerant?*"

It is eloquent testimony to the strength of the convention that prevented the nineteenth-century woman from public lecturing that not one of those female abolitionists, so intrepid in the presence of a mob, could bring herself to speak in any formal gathering. The councils of the Anti-Slavery Society were guided again and again by the wisdom of Mrs. Chapman, Mrs. Follen, and Mrs. Child, but never by their voices. The Reverend Samuel May tells how he repeatedly sprang to the platform, "crying, 'Hear me as the mouthpiece of Mrs. Child, or Mrs. Chapman, or Mrs. Follen,' and convulsed the audience with a stroke of wit, or electrified them with a flash of eloquence, caught from the lips of one or the other of our anti-slavery prophetesses."

It was not until 1838 that Maria Child altered her convictions on feminine oratory. When Angelina Grimké felt impelled to break the bonds of silence and address a committee of the Massachusetts Legislature on her experience as a slaveholder, Maria Child accompanied her to the State House and wrote to her friend E. Carpenter: "I think it was a spectacle of the greatest moral sublimity I ever witnessed." She herself never felt called upon to speak for the cause; her talent for persuasion worked most effectively in another medium.

The *Appeal* was followed by book after abolitionist book. Repetitive only in their ultimate purpose and the quiet objectivity of their manner, they presented their case in a diversity of ways from a variety of angles. Between 1833 and 1836 Maria Child published *The Oasis,* an anti-slavery miscellany; an *Anti-Slavery Catechism,* which furnished answers to the questions she was most often asked by her friends; *Authentic Anecdotes of Slavery;* and *The Evils of Slavery and the Cure of Slavery,* the First Proved by the Opinions of Southerners Themselves, the Last Shown by Historical Evidence. And while she wrote this clear and factual propaganda she was engaged in the composition of her most transcendental novel, *Philothea,* a romance of the time of Pericles and Aspasia.

This dichotomy of mind was characteristic. Whittier said that her mysticism and her realism ran in close parallel lines and certainly she moved easily from one to the other. By choice she would have remained, like Margaret Fuller, an artist working on the ideal plane, out of the heat and dust of reform, working, to be sure, for the improvement of mankind but by ministry to the soul and the intellect, not to the body. She would have liked to do more novels like *Philothea,* more short stories like her famous "Children of Mt. Ida," more essays like "What Is Beauty?" published (April, 1843) in the *Dial,* but the power of her Puritan ancestors was strong; she could not pass by on the other side of a duty waiting to be done and her observant imagination saw duties everywhere.

The practical tendencies of the age [she wrote in the preface to *Philothea*], and particularly of the country in which I lived, have so continually forced me into the actual, that my mind has seldom obtained freedom to rise into the ideal. The hope of extended usefulness has hitherto induced a strong effort to throw myself into the spirit of the times; which is prone to neglect beautiful and fragrant flowers, unless their roots will answer for vegetables, and their leaves for herbs.

Such homely, pungent metaphors, generated by bondage to the actual, are frequent in her prose, giving it much of its vigor and originality. This, for instance, in the *Anti-Slavery Standard* (May 27, 1841):

He [Channing], and other champions of what is called individual action, will not admit my proposition, because they will not perceive it to be true; but, the simple fact is, anti-slavery societies are the steam, and they are the passengers in the cars. They may not like the puffing and blowing, the cinders and the jolting; but the powerful agency carries them onward.

Yet *Philothea,* the escape novel, is written with great charm and is far more skillfully composed than the early books though the plot melodrama is still thick. The background is carefully got up and the historical personages speak in character—Plato, for instance, quotes liberally from his Dialogues—yet contemporary critics found the atmosphere more redolent of Cambridge than of Athens.

Greek or Boston, talk of the soul in relation to the gods was a refreshment to Maria Child. So was the contemplation of the beautiful objects, the purple robes, the marble statues, the golden lyres, with which she could surround her Athenian characters. The still-life passages in her fiction are always written *con amore.* Even in the New England novels she manages to introduce here and there a pearl-set miniature or an elegant workbox and in *Philothea* she could let her imagination run. Though quite untaught in the arts, always too poor to fulfill her dream of European travel, she had an instinctive delight in line and pattern.

I have a little plaster figure of a caryatid, which acts upon my spirit like a magician's spell. . . . to me it has an expression of the highest kind. Repose after conflict—not the repose of innocence, but the repose of wisdom. Many a time this hard summer I have laid down dish-cloth or broom and gone to refresh my spirit by gazing on it a few minutes. (To Francis G. Shaw, Northampton, 1840.)

She looked at nature with the same delight—bare boughs against the sky, a briar rose in the dooryard—enjoying not so much God's immanence, though she was always aware of that, as his craftsman's skill in harmony and design.

In the year *Philothea* was published David Child set out on another expedition in helmet, shield, and chain armor: a three-year task of infinite labor and no possible profit to himself but of potentially great usefulness to the slave.

A problem which constantly troubled the early abolitionists was the discovery of substitutes for commodities —cotton and sugar in particular—which could be produced economically only by slave labor. Many ardent souls took, and kept, vows to wear no cotton garment and to drink their tea unsweetened but they knew well that only a handful of the devoted would follow them to these extremes. If, though, adequate substitutes could be offered for the products of slavery many thoughtful Northerners would gladly use them. One of the most promising possibilities was the replacing of cane with beet sugar. Beet sugar had been made in Europe since 1802 and Napoleon had established a profitable industry in France but nothing at all about the process was known in the United States. Should not someone go abroad to study it and then attempt the manufacture in America? A small fund was raised for the purpose and David Child undertook the quest. He had no agricultural training but he did know something of Europe and European tongues and he had the scholar's ability to learn a new thing.

The outset of the journey was painful. David Child was mysteriously arrested on the dock in New York on the flimsy grounds of an old debt. This is the only occasion on record when his wife's spirit failed her; Maria Child sat down on a pile of luggage and burst into tears. But she did not weep long; she was soon packing up a bundle of clothing for her husband to take to prison and comforting him there until well-to-do friends could arrange for his release.

The European voyage meant for the Childs a long separation, eighteen months, but so much was accomplished that they were happy about it in the end. David Child visited sugar factories in France, Belgium, and Germany; he talked with beet cultivators and sugar manufacturers distinguished for their science and their success; he read everything that had been printed on the subject; and he came home an expert. The Connecticut River Valley, it was decided, offered the best opportunity for the anti-slavery experiment so the Childs spent the next year and a half in Northampton, Massachusetts, not altogether happily. David Child's agricultural ideas seemed to the neighboring farmers thoroughly impractical. He found them skeptical and not at all cooperative while his wife was discouraged by their obtuseness in abolition matters and by their religious bigotry.

If I were to choose my home [she wrote her brother December 22, 1838], I certainly would not place it in the Valley of the Connecticut. It is true, the river is broad and clear, the hills majestic, and the whole aspect of outward nature most lovely. But oh! the narrowness, the bigotry of man! To think of hearing a whole family vie with each other, in telling of vessels that were wrecked, or shattered, or delayed on their passage, because they sailed on Sunday! To think of people's troubling their heads with the question whether the thief could have been instantaneously converted on the cross, so that the Saviour could promise him an entrance to Paradise! In an age of such stirring inquiry, and of such extended benevolence—in a world which requires all the efforts of the good and wise merely to make it receptive of holy influences, what a pity it is that so much intellect should be wasted upon such theological jargon!

Despite the self-righteousness of Northampton there was much agricultural curiosity in the country at large and the experiment proved a scientific if not a financial success. David Child demonstrated that the cultivation of the beet and the manufacture of beet sugar were perfectly practicable in America and he put the results of his demonstration into an excellent pamphlet on which the Massachusetts Agricultural Society bestowed a premium. Unfortunately beet sugar manufacture to be profitable has to be carried on on a much greater scale than the funds for the Northampton experiment permitted. It was not until five years after the Civil War that the first successful American beet sugar factory was built, in California.

The work in Northampton furnished the Childs with house and food but little besides, and the writing which they both did for anti-slavery periodicals brought them of course more merit than cash. Something to provide a regular income had to be done so, in the spring of 1841, Maria Child agreed to undertake the editorship of the

National Anti-Slavery Standard, a weekly paper which the Anti-Slavery Society had initiated in New York the year before. A measure of the distance the abolitionists moved in advance of their time is the fact that they could take the revolutionary step of appointing a woman to the editorship of a reform journal (seven years before Jane Swisshelm's *Saturday Visiter*) without either controversy or apology. It was simply announced that

We greatly rejoice . . . not merely that we have her extraordinary ability and faithfulness enlisted, and her reputation *invested* in the cause—but that they come to our aid in the form of *woman*. It will, we anticipate, prove an era in our enterprise. Woman has spoken and written in the anti-slavery service, but this is, we believe, her first assumption of the editorial chair in this great movement.

Even this seemed to Maria Child too much feminism.

I am heartily obliged to brother Rogers [she wrote in her first editorial] for his friendly greeting and cordial welcome. . . .

In answer to his wish, that I should on this occasion, "forget every incident of my existence, except my humanity," I merely reply that I would *he*, too, had forgotten all else.

Had Mr. Child's business made it possible for him to remove to New York, his experience in editing, his close observation of public affairs, and the general character of his mind, would have made it far better for the cause to have him for a resident, and myself for an assistant editor, but in any other point of view, it is quite unimportant that the arrangement is reversed.

David Child sent frequent contributions from Northampton and occasionally was able to share the editorial duties in New York. It was at this time, too, that he did his most distinguished scholarly labor for the cause, the collection and arrangement of the arguments against the admission of Texas which J. Q. Adams made the basis of his speeches during the debates in Congress.

Maria Child, entering upon her new duties, found herself "a sort of black sheep," as she said, among the New York literary and editorial fraternity. As an abolition editor she could get no courtesies from booksellers, had difficulty in borrowing from club libraries, and found the task of gathering information and preparing extracts far more onerous than she had anticipated. "The type is fine, and that large sheet [it was the largest of all the abolition journals] swallows an incredible amount of matter." Much of the paper she wrote herself, including every week two or three vigorous editorials.

She had accepted the position for a year but she stayed actually for three; the Society would not let her go. As Wendell Phillips wrote her in 1842, "the *ultra*, the moderate, the half-converted, the zealous, the indifferent, the active, all welcome the *Standard*, and . . . it is fast changing them all into its own likeness of sound, liberal, generous, active, devoted men and women."

During her years in New York Maria Child lived most happily in the house of the good Quaker Isaac Hopper, one of the most original and competent reformers of that great reforming generation. The "true life" of *Isaac T. Hopper* which she published in 1854 (two years after her friend's death) is unconventional biography of a very agreeable kind. A long series of anti-slavery adventures are set down as she heard Friend Hopper tell them on summer evening walks along the Bowery or on winter nights beside the family fire; from the cumulative anecdotes emerges a firm and individual figure, the stalwart Quaker, full of courage and ingenious resource, who fought persistently from boyhood to old age, in the cause of the oppressed, risking his means, his reputation, and more than once his life, yet never transgressing the principles of antiviolence. "If thou wert not a coward," he said on one occasion to an angry slave catcher, "thou wouldst not try to intimidate me with a pistol. I do not believe thou hast the least intention of using it in any other way; but thou art much agitated, and may fire it accidentally; therefore I request thee not to point it toward me, but to turn it the other way."

When another ruffian, to prove the identity of a fugitive by the whip scars on his body, ordered the man to strip and let the court examine his back, Friend Hopper objected: " 'Thou hast produced no evidence that the man thou hast arrested is a slave,' said he. 'Thou and he are on the same footing before this court. We have as good a right to examine thy back, as we have to examine his.' He added, with a very significant tone, 'In some places, they whip for kidnapping.' "

Isaac Hopper was so well versed in the law and so ingenious in turning his knowledge to account, that he often extricated a slave by some perfectly legal twist which neither magistrate nor lawyer could contest. If that failed he was adroit in throwing the pursuers off the scent or in spiriting the fugitive away.

"Don't get frightened when the right moment comes to act; but keep thy wits about thee, and do as I tell thee. Thy master will come here tomorrow at ten o'clock, according to appointment. I must deliver thee up to him, and receive back the obligation for one thousand dollars, which I have given him. Do thou stand with thy back against the door, which opens from this room into the parlor. When he has returned the paper to me, open the door quickly, lock it on the inside, and run through the parlor into the back-yard. There is a wall there eight feet high, with spikes at the top. Thou wilt find a clothes-horse leaning against it, to help thee up. When thou hast mounted, kick the clothes-horse down behind thee, drop on the other side of the wall, and be off."

In the forty years of his residence in Philadelphia, Friend Hopper estimated for Maria Child, he gave aid to more than a thousand fugitives and his benevolence was by no means confined to the slave; "wherever there was good to be done, his heart and hand were ready." He believed, as Maria Child herself believed, that to see a need was to be called upon to fill it.

If a hundred citizens in New-York would act as Friend Hopper did, the evil [in this case the exclusion of Negroes from public conveyances] would soon be remedied. It is the almost universal failure in individual duty, which so accumulates errors and iniquities in society, that the ultra-theories, and extra efforts of reformers become absolutely necessary to prevent the balance of things from being destroyed; as thunder and lightning are required to purify a poluted atmosphere.

In Philadelphia Isaac Hopper served as a prison inspector and in New York, where he removed in 1829 to conduct a bookshop for the Hicksite Quakers, he was agent for the Prison Association formed to find employment for released criminals to whom respectable folk were often reluctant to give work. Maria Child could have had no better guide to the miseries and the alleviating charities of the great city which she learned to know far more intimately than most of its lifetime inhabitants. She was soon involved in endless personal, in addition to her professional, good works for she had a capacity for inviting confidence. All sorts of people would talk to her, not just because she was compassionate and wise but because she was interested; about life in any form she had indefatigable curiosity. This is the trait that Lowell makes play with in the *Fable for Critics* where "Philothea"—she and "Miranda" Fuller are the only ladies present—comes in "with her face all aglow,"

She has just been dividing some poor creature's woe,
And can't tell which pleases her most, to relieve
His wants, or his story to hear and believe;
No doubt against many deep griefs she prevails,
For her ear is the refuge of destitute tales;
She knows well that silence is sorrow's best food,
And that talking draws off from the heart its black blood,
So she'll listen with patience and let you unfold
Your bundle of rags as 't were pure cloth of gold,
Which, indeed, it all turns to as soon as she's touched it,
And (to borrow a phrase from the nursery) *muched* it.

Many of the stories poured out to her Maria Child transmuted as propaganda for the Anti-Slavery Society or the Prison Association, sometimes in their regular journals, sometimes in popular magazines which did not object to a little reform if it was well trimmed with melodrama or sentiment or morality. There was, for instance, the story of "Charity Bowery," set down almost precisely in her own words. Charity did washing for Mrs. Child in New York and told her how she had obtained her freedom and managed to buy one of her sixteen children and how she had sent word to her old mistress, who refused to let her purchase her little grandson, to "prepare to meet poor Charity at the judgment seat." Or "The Irish Heart," the case of a reformed convict from the files of the Prison Assocation, for Philothea could transmute from cold print as effectively as from firsthand confidence. Or the account, given her by the husband of Harriet Beecher Stowe, of "The Emancipated Slaveholders," who never themselves knew freedom till they set their bondsmen free.

Many of the heroines of these stories are prostitutes, in whom Mrs. Child's interest went deeper than the romantic pity common to the literary ladies of her generation. She was concerned to discover the social, and particularly the psychological, causes of their fall and, though presented in the language of sentiment, her diagnosis is usually scientific and sound. "Elizabeth Wilson," for instance, hanged for infanticide. As a child she was "always caressing her kitten, or twining her arms about [her brother] Willie's neck, or leaning on her mother's lap, begging for a kiss." When she was ten her mother died and the sight of the corpse "with large coins on the eye-lids, was so awfully impressed on her imagination, that the image followed her everywhere, even into her dreams." Elizabeth's father was kind but undemonstrative; her stepmother, cold. She was bound out to service, separated from her beloved Willie, treated, not cruelly, but entirely without understanding—and so, even to the lady subscribers to the *Columbian Magazine*, Elizabeth's ardent response to the affection of a handsome stranger seemed not so much wicked as inevitable. Mrs. Child had dusted another mirror.

Some of these golden tales made their first appearance

in the columns of the *Anti-Slavery Standard* and it was for those columns also, and at the same time for the Boston *Courier*, that Mrs. Child began the *Letters from New York* which, collected between covers, made the most admired of all her books. "Really, a contribution to American literature," Margaret Fuller called it in the *Dial*. The *Letters* are also Maria Child's most characteristic work. The parallel lines of realism and idealism run here very close together and the writer steps easily back and forth. Taking off from something she has noticed as she walked down Broadway or strolled on the Bowery or crossed on the ferry to Brooklyn, she lets her thought or her fancy run. The fancy runs usually too fast and far for modern taste, is too heavily loaded with violets and rainbows, gauze-winged fairies and Swedenborgian "correspondences," but the thought is almost always interesting:

Of brick walls, for instance, glaring in the August sun:

Strange to say, they are *painted* red, blocked off with white compartments, as numerous as Protestant sects, and as unlovely in their narrowness. What an expenditure for ugliness and discomfort to the eye! To paint bricks their own colour, resembles the great outlay of time and money in theological schools, to enable dismal, arbitrary souls to give an approved image of themselves in their ideas of Deity.

Of a fire in her neighborhood:

A single bucket of water, thrown on immediately, would have extinguished it; but it was not instantly perceived, roofs were dry, and the wind was blowing a perfect March gale. Like slavery in our government, it was not put out in the day of small beginnings, and so went on increasing in its rage, making a deal of hot and disagreeable work.

Of lion-taming:

The menagerie attracts crowds daily. It is certainly exciting to see Driesbach dash across the arena in his chariot drawn by lions; or sleep on a bed of living leopards, with a crouching tiger for his pillow; or offering his hand to the mouth of a panther, as he would to the caresses of a kitten. But I could not help questioning whether it were right for a man to risk so much, or for animals to suffer so much, for the purposes of amusement and pecuniary profit.

No matter where the theme carries her she speaks always as though she were writing a personal letter, to a definite individual, or as though she were talking to a companion during a walk, pointing excitedly and saying, See. This must have been the tone of the conversation her friends enjoyed so much. New York interested her endlessly yet she never really liked it. She was by nature a country dweller, troubled by noise and crowds, and beyond that she had a deep distaste for the lusty commercialism of the day, seeing it not as an example of exuberant American energy but as the destroyer of all impulses to beauty, the negation of philosophy and art, with Wall Street as its culmination.

For all their quality of direct address the *Letters from New York* have none of the rush of noise and chatter which fills such columns as Grace Greenwood's and those of most of the newspaper correspondents of the day. Events held for Maria Child comparatively little interest; what concerned her were people, places, objects, and their intellectual and spiritual ramifications. "Some of her magazine papers," wrote Poe in his "Literati," "are distinguished for graceful and brilliant imagination—a quality rarely noticed in our countrywomen."

With one of the great crusades of the day which began during her years as editor, the woman's suffrage movement, Maria Child had no immediate connection. Her hands were more than filled with tasks and the ballot interested her only as a means to other work. Yet the suffragists thought of her always as a fellow laborer and a forerunner. The Gage-Stanton History of the suffrage movement is dedicated to a score of brave women who broke the first paths for their sex and the list begins: Mary Wollstonecraft, Frances Wright, Lucretia Mott, Harriet Martineau, Lydia Maria Child. The History records further Mrs. Child's legacy of $1,000 for the work of the Suffrage Society, the first such bequest ever made. It publishes also various characteristic letters which she wrote to be read at suffrage conventions:

Dear Mrs. Stanton: . . . What I most wish for women is that they should go right ahead, and do whatever they can do well, without talking about it. But the false position in which they are placed by the laws and customs of society, renders it almost impossible that they should be sufficiently independent to do whatever they can do well, unless the world approves of it. They need a great deal of talking to, to make them aware that they are in fetters. Therefore I say, success to your Convention, and to all similiar ones!

In 1852 David and Maria Child settled in Wayland, then a remote little village connected with Boston only by a daily stagecoach. Mrs. Child's father had purchased a house there which he shared with them until his death in 1856, an agreeable old house with an elm and a willow before its door and a prospect of green meadows sloping down to the Sudbury River. The years in Wayland—

they lived there the rest of their lives—were quiet, laborious, frugal, but productive years and very happy.

David Child never succeeded in getting the federal appointment for which he hoped but he wrote much for the anti-slavery cause and took his share of tasks about the house and garden. His wife speaks of his continual reading and study and records her dependence on "his richly stored mind, which was able and ready to furnish needed information on any subject. He was my walking dictionary of many languages, my Universal Encyclopedia."

It was she who managed the financial as well as the domestic affairs of the household; she who brought in what little income they had and determined how it should be spent. It is she always of whom reminiscent visitors—for friends came despite the distance—write with enthusiasm. The simple house had individuality and charm. There was always good talk there and a generous hospitality though the fare was very plain. Maria Child gave so freely of everything she possessed that all her life long she was poorer and less comfortable than she need have been. Her "habits of observation" showed her so clearly the good her money could do that she found it continually necessary to give out of all proportion to her means. Wendell Phillips, who managed her business affairs, tells of saying to her when she asked him at some exigency in the freedmen's cause to send them for her a hundred dollars, " 'I do not think, Mrs. Child, you can afford to give so much just now.' . . . 'Well,' she answered, 'I will think it over, and send you word tomorrow.' Tomorrow word came, 'Please send them two hundred.' "

The wealthy friends who tried to help her she resisted affectionately but with an independent pride. When one of them wanted to settle on her a sum that would bring in several thousand a year she firmly declined, till Wendell Phillips suggested that perhaps her friend had difficulty in distributing her income wisely and Mrs. Child ought to be willing to help. She thereupon accepted the trust and portioned out every dollar of income to the causes in which she believed. In the same spirit she never hesitated to importune her friends and acquaintances for worthy organizations or individual cases of need, exerting her propaganda skill in persuasive letters until her end was accomplished.

Her own expenditures she kept to the barest minimum. The house was plainly furnished; all domestic labor she performed herself; meals were wholesome but very simple; and her dress was so inexpensive and unadorned that its lack of fashion was apparent even to her masculine friends. In the later portraits her only ornaments are a small white collar and a neat cap tied under her chin, but the face it circles is singularly attractive though it has no pretension to beauty. The mouth is too long and straight, the nose too broad, the chin too wide and firm, but the eyes are wise and merry and the whole expression is an agreeable combination of vitality and serenity. Her hair she wore parted in the middle and drawn smoothly back, not, as the usual fashion was, over the ears but looped around them. The portraits of Margaret Fuller show the same rather unattractive style and one imagines that the two young intellectuals had agreed on the compromise because they felt that listening was so important a part of life.

The seclusion of Wayland made possible the completion in 1855 of a work Maria Child had begun in the New

York days and planned long before that, *The Progress of Religious Ideas through Successive Ages*. The cost of publishing the three volumes she bore herself and she realized, as she had anticipated, only a trifling profit but it seemed to her important at any price to bear witness to her religious tenets as it was important to speak her convictions on racial discrimination. Her purpose, she said, was a very simple one: "to show that *theology* is not *religion*." "I would candidly advise," the preface begins "persons who are conscious of bigoted attachment to any creed, or theory, not to purchase this book. Whether they are bigoted Christians, or bigoted infidels, its tone will be likely to displease them."

Displeasure was a euphemism for what she expected, and got. "This is the second time," she wrote to Lucy Osgood, "I have walked out in stormy weather without a cloak." From her youth up she had felt that the descriptions by Christian writers of other forms of religious faith were eminently unfair; she thought that readers should be given the facts and left to their own conclusions, but to do this it was necessary, as she said, to trample under her feet a deal of theological underbrush.

Her own intensely religious nature had never been able to confine itself within the bonds of even the broadest sect. A creed to Maria Child was always the hardened shell of what had been a living truth. She could not act within it. She coveted the strength and happiness of religious communion with her fellows but even her admired brother and his fellow Unitarians, many of whose ideas she shared, and the Quakers, to whom she was close spiritual kin, seemed to her at times unduly narrow and stiff. She could not reconcile herself to any limitation of her own spiritual insights. These came to her often through the arts, especially music which, though she was technically quite ignorant, moved her often to illuminating ecstasy. Her tireless interest also in all forms of experience led her to concern herself with table rappings and the other phenomena of spiritualism, with cases of thought transference and of second sight, but this interest was not, as some of her friends supposed, mere enthusiastic credulity. Lowell was amusing but wrong when, playing on her admiration for Ole Bull, he said that

> She has such a musical taste, she will go
> Any distance to hear one who draws a long bow.

Actually she was not credulous but curious, focusing on the spirit world the observant attention and analysis by which she had sought the true remedy for slavery or the best method of reforming criminals. As the imaginative inquiring mind of today thinks to come at the secret of creation by the discovery of a new isotope so, a century ago, it sought a clue in the "electric fluid" by which human mind was supposed to communicate with mind. To an age witnessing such miraculous developments in earthly communication as the railway and the telegraph, it seemed quite probable that swifter and clearer means of spiritual communication might be discovered. Many of the phenomena of the relations between minds and between mind and body with which Maria Child tried to deal are now the commonplaces of psychology. That she and other strong-minded women were interested in dreams and phrenology, in mesmerism and spirit rappings is a definite indication not of weakness but of mental vigor and courage.

Maria Child's interest in the phenomena of spiritism was strengthened by her own acute sensitivity to the emotions and experiences of her friends.

The outrage upon Charles Sumner made me literally ill for several days. It brought on nervous headache and painful suffocations about the heart. If I could only have done something, it would have loosened that tight ligature that seemed to stop the flowing of my blood. But I never was one who knew how to serve the Lord by standing and waiting; and to stand and wait then! (To Mrs. S. B. Shaw, 1856.)

This same finely tuned imagination turned upon John Brown produced, quite without calculated intention, Maria Child's most dramatic and famous piece of propaganda. She had never met Brown personally but had of course closely followed his career through Garrison and other abolitionist friends, had even shared in it to some extent by dashing off for the *Tribune* in 1856 a serial propaganda story called "The Kansas Immigrants." When the news came of the raid at Harper's Ferry, Maria Child though distressed by the act of violence was deeply moved by the courage and high idealism which prompted it. She felt, as she had when Sumner was beaten, that she could not endure to stand and wait, she must do something for the old hero lying wounded in hostile hands. To the group of Boston abolitionists excitedly discussing the situation she made a suggestion which they approved. She sent a letter to Governor Wise of Virginia and one to Captain Brown.

Wayland, Oct. 26, 1859

Dear Captain Brown: Though personally unknown to you, you will recognize in my name an earnest friend of Kansas, when circumstances made that Territory the battle-ground between the antagonistic principles of slavery and freedom, which politicians so vainly strive to reconcile in the government of the United States.

Believing in peace principles, I cannot sympathize with the method you chose to advance the cause of freedom. But I honor your generous intentions,—I admire your courage, moral and physical. I reverence you for the humanity which tempered your zeal. I sympathize with you in your cruel bereavement, your sufferings, and your wrongs. In brief, I love you and bless you.

Thousands of hearts are throbbing with sympathy as warm as mine. I think of you night and day, bleeding in prison, surrounded by hostile faces, sustained only by trust in God and your own strong heart. I long to nurse you—to speak to you sisterly words of sympathy and consolation. I have asked permission of Governor Wise to do so. If the request is not granted, I cherish the hope that these few words may at least reach your hands, and afford you some little solace. May you be strengthened by the conviction that no honest man ever sheds blood for freedom in vain, however much he may be mistaken in his efforts. May God sustain you, and carry you through whatsoever may be in store for you! Yours, with heartfelt respect, sympathy and affection,

L. Maria Child

The letter was an impulse of pure humanity. Mrs. Child had no intention of making her scheme public but packed her little trunk, collected a quantity of old linen for lint, and waited only a reply from Governor Wise to whom she had written for permission to proceed.

The Governor answered that of course she had every right to visit Virginia and that he would protect her passage but he suggested "the imprudence of risking any experiment upon the peace of a society very much excited by the crimes with whose chief author you seem to sympathize so much." Word came at the same time that Brown's wife had been able to go to him and Mrs. Child's project was therefore abandoned but she turned it to account for the cause. She sent to Wise's plausible letter a long and acute reply explaining why he seemed to her hypocritical, presenting him, in a form he could not choose but read, with a kind of condensed version of her *Appeal* on behalf of the Africans. She did not expect her letter to circulate beyond the gubernatorial circle but it aroused so much talk there that someone passed it on to the New York *Tribune*, to which she then thought proper to send her letter to John Brown and his grateful reply. The *Tribune* publication of these documents called forth a long letter of reproach from a lady of Virginia, Mrs. M. J. C. Mason, wife of the senator who drew the Fugitive Slave Law.

Do you read your Bible, Mrs. Child? [the letter began.] If you do, read there, "Woe to you hypocrites," and take to yourself with twofold damnation that terrible sentence; . . . *You* would soothe with sisterly and motherly care the hoary-headed murderer of Harper's Ferry! . . . Now, compare yourself with those your "sympathy" would devote to such ruthless ruin, and say, on that "word of honor, which never has been broken," would *you* stand by the bedside of an old negro, dying of a hopeless disease, to alleviate his suffering as far as human aid could? Have *you* ever watched the last, lingering illness of a consumptive, to soothe, as far as in you lay, the inevitable fate? Do *you* soften the pangs of maternity in those around you by all the care and comfort you can give? . . . I will add, in conclusion, no Southerner ought, after your letter to Governor Wise and to Brown, to read a line of your composition, or to touch a magazine which bears your name in its list of contributors; and in this we hope for the "sympathy" at least of those at the North who deserve the name of woman.

Mrs. Mason underestimated her antagonist. Mrs. Child was practiced in the refutation of just such stubbornly provincial arguments. She had done it often calmly; she wrote now at white heat and so effectively that the pamphlet, into which the whole correspondence was immediately gathered, became a highly useful abolition document. Three hundred thousand copies were sold and one phrase in particular was quoted again and again and again. "It would be extremely difficult to find any woman in our villages who does *not* sew for the poor, and watch with the sick, whenever occasion requires. . . . I have never known an instance where the 'pangs of maternity' did not meet with requisite assistance; and here at the North, after we have helped the mothers, *we do not sell the babies.*"

Pacifist as she was, the declaration of war was to Maria Child a cause for sadness; the preservation of the Union did not seem sufficient cause for slaughter and she was horrified by the army's care to treat the flying slave as Southern property which should not be confiscated but returned.

January 21, 1862:—This winter I have for the first time been knitting for the army; but I do it only for Kansas troops. I can trust them, for they have vowed a vow unto the Lord that no fugitive shall ever be surrendered in their camps.

It was not until the signing of the Emancipation Proclamation that she felt the combat justified.

"Contrabands Coming into Camp in Consequence of the Proclamation," drawn by A. R. Waud

And with the freeing of the slaves she found at once other work to do. The Negro now had liberty but very little else; he needed work, money, education, friends, and to all these Maria Child tried to help him. She contributed steadily to the Freedmen's Aid Association, giving always, as we have seen, far beyond her means. She wrote more of her persuasive letters, picturing so vividly individual cases of need that the recipient could not deny the assistance or the funds she asked. She prepared and published (1865) at her own expense a *Freedmen's Book* which offered to the newly liberated slave practical advice and spiritual encouragement, not at all in the tone of a tract but in the language of a friendly serious conversation. Some of the stories and verses are by other hands but a large part of the book she wrote herself alternating biographical sketches of heroic Negroes with paragraphs of practical advice on health, dress, economy, or education.

Most vigorously of all Maria Child worked for a principle which even the North barely understood and seldom practiced: racial equality.

"Our cause," she had written of abolition in 1861, "is going to mount the throne of popular favor. Then I shall bid good-by to it, and take hold of something else that is unpopular. I never work on the winning side."

Actually she had not waited for the success of abolition to espouse her new unpopular cause. She had been aware of the need for preaching racial tolerance when she first entered the anti-slavery ranks with the *Appeal*. Its last chapter is concerned with "Prejudices against People of Color, and Our Duties in Relation to This Subject," of which she had said roundly: "Let us not flatter ourselves that we are in reality any better than our brethren of the

South. Thanks to our soil and climate, and the early exertions of the Quakers, the *form* of slavery does not exist among us; but the very *spirit* of the hateful and mischievous thing is here in all its strength." Directly and indirectly she now labored this point in her letters to the press and she made it the theme of the last and most interesting of her novels.

A Romance of the Republic, published in 1867, is dedicated to the Father and Mother of Colonel Shaw of whom she once wrote to Whittier: "I have always thought that no incident in the anti-slavery conflict, including the war, was at once so sublime and romantic as Robert G. Shaw riding through Washington Street at the head of that black regiment."

The heroines of the tale are the incredibly beautiful daughters of a New Orleans merchant and a Spanish West-Indian Negress. Their father, who is devoted to them, brings them up in luxury and seclusion but neglects to manumit them and is carried off suddenly by death. After extraordinary adventures and escapes the elder sister becomes an opera singer and both find adoring husbands to whom their black blood is a matter of complete indifference. The story runs on into the second generation and through the Civil War. The plot is a web of coincidences and melodramatic elements: wounded heroes, wicked seducers, false marriages, faithful servants, Italian music masters, even children changed at birth, but within this thicket the characters move and talk like human beings. One becomes attached to them and concerned about their destinies; that society should classify some of them as white and others as black seems altogether arbitrary and meaningless; the point of racial equality is made both directly and indirectly. In 1868 *An Appeal for the Indians* attacked another facet of the problem.

Through the remaining years of her life Maria Child continued to work for this and the other causes which seemed to her good. At seventy-six she published yet another book, *Aspirations of the World,* an anthology designed to show that in fundamental religious matters there is much on which all men agree. So full of projects and activity was all her old age that there was small space for the usual looking back but when she did, it was most often to the early years of the abolition struggle, those years when "The Holy Spirit did actually descend upon men and women in tongues of flame. . . . All suppression of selfishness makes the moment great; and mortals were never more sublimely forgetful of self than were the abolitionists in those early days."

"Industry Conquers Everything"

BIBLIOGRAPHICAL NOTE

In addition to their own writings, the principal sources of information about the ladies discussed in this book are these. (There is no book on Grace Greenwood.)

Catharine Beecher

Mae Elizabeth Harveson, *Catharine Esther Beecher, Pioneer Educator*, Philadelphia, 1932.

Lyman Beecher Stowe, "Catharine Beecher," *Saints, Sinners and Beechers*, Indianapolis, 1934.

Amelia Bloomer

D. C. Bloomer, *Life and Writings of Amelia Bloomer*, Boston, 1895.

Philip D. Jordan, "The Bloomers in Iowa," *The Palimpsest*, September 1939, State Historical Society of Iowa, Iowa City.

Maria Child

Letters of Lydia Maria Child, with a Biographical Introduction by John G. Whittier and an Appendix by Wendell Phillips, Boston, 1883.

Louisa McCord

Jessie M. Fraser, *Louisa C. McCord*, Bulletin of the University of South Carolina, No. 91, Columbia, 1920.

Louisa McCord Smythe, *For Old Lang Syne*, privately printed, Charleston, 1900.

Jane Swisshelm

Arthur J. Larsen, ed., *Crusader and Feminist*, Letters of Jane Grey Swisshelm, Minnesota Historical Society, Saint Paul, 1934.